THE GARDEN AT
HIGHGROVE

THE GARDEN AT
HIGHGROVE

H.R.H. THE PRINCE OF WALES
AND CANDIDA LYCETT GREEN

PHOTOGRAPHY BY
ANDREW LAWSON AND
CHRISTOPHER SIMON SYKES

St. Martin's Press New York

Contents

Introduction

by H.R.H. The Prince of Wales

PEOPLE OFTEN ASK ME why it was that I came to live at Highgrove. Having lived here for the past twenty years, I have come to the conclusion that it must have been because I had a subconscious urge to enhance the existing, but somewhat featureless, landscape and to provide the house with a more appropriate setting. I suppose I could have gone on searching for the perfect house and garden – a combination of other people's dreams and ideas – but I relished the challenge of starting with a blank canvas and seeing if I could fulfil my own dreams for the garden.

At the same time I remember feeling deeply about the rampant destruction that had been wreaked on the countryside, in the name of progress, throughout the 1960s and 1970s. The grubbing up of miles of hedges, the loss of ancient woodland, the draining of water meadows, the ploughing up of chalk grassland, the excessive use of chemicals on both farm land and gardens. I remember longing to heal the countryside; to bind up its wounds and to re-clothe it in its rightful form. So much about modern farming and gardening seemed to consist of a furious battle waged against Nature which, in my heart of hearts, I felt could only end in tears as Nature never allows us to have anything for nothing. For this reason I felt an irresistible desire to work in harmony with Nature and thereby to accept the inevitable limits to 'perfection' that such a desire would impose.

Of course, trying to translate a series of rather vague feelings into practical, organic action was considerably more challenging than I thought. For instance, it took me quite some time to realize that certain varieties of plant or tree are more resistant to disease than others and therefore are better suited to an organic system. Dealing with slug damage to hostas was another interesting complication but, in the long term, it is infinitely satisfying when you begin to see the beneficial effects on the bird population and on the general health of the soil. On this basis, even the extra weeds can become almost bearable.

Having abandoned the 'quick-fix' approach to dealing with problems in the garden, I began to discover how to adopt a philosophical approach instead. Gradually I realized that each year is different and that the same problems rarely occur two years running. I also discovered the definite advantages of creating my own compost and eliminating unnecessary waste, not to mention the fascination of unearthing traditional systems of management which were rashly abandoned in the rush to adopt the latest fashion in invasive horticultural technology. When all is said and done, I believe it is still worth recalling some of the hard-won wisdom accumulated over centuries in terms of how to work with the grain of Nature rather than against it.

Throughout the entire process of developing the garden at Highgrove I have striven to create a physical reflection of what I feel at a much deeper level. Although I wanted each area of the garden to have its own atmosphere, I hoped that, when they were linked together, the different parts might create an integrated experience that would warm the heart, feed the soul and delight the eye. To do this, I felt it was vital to have a series of features that would 'anchor' the garden to the landscape. Hedges, I felt, were essential to provide form and structure, let alone windbreaks. Likewise, vistas terminated by 'eye catchers' such as a dovecote or a column at the end of an avenue, or a glimpse of a building like the Sanctuary through a gap in the trees, were crucial to the integrity of the 'picture' I wanted to create. In this sense the genius of William Kent, as demonstrated at Rousham or Houghton, has been my inspiration. And so, incidentally, has been that of Lawrence Johnston at Hidcote. Above all, I felt it was important to link the house intimately with the garden and to ensure that out of every window was a view to catch, and hold, the eye. To hold the eye by leading it on through the subtle exploitation of the foreground and background seems to me the exciting challenge when trying to unite house and garden as part of a seamless tapestry.

Having 'painted in' the main structure of the garden on my blank canvas, I shall probably finish my days happily 'filling in details'. I have reached the stage where I realize how many mistakes I have made in the development of the garden and am now trying to put them right. A garden is a constantly evolving thing and I find that wherever I go in the world a new inspiration will come to me, or as I walk around the garden a further refinement will suggest itself. I have already reorganized the Sundial Garden, which has become a black and white garden. Who knows what it may become in years ahead? Likewise, I have recently designed a Box Garden, out of what used to be optimistically called the Butterfly Garden, thus confusing my poor garden guides. As time goes on, I shall certainly pursue my ambition to search for a model of sustainability in both the garden and on the farm in an effort to engender the kind of environmental and social benefits that may prove to be of some value to those who come after me, and who may face untold challenges in an over-pressurized world.

It may sound strange to some, but I thank the Good Lord that I have been spared so far to see the results of the past twenty years and to sit in the shade of some of the trees that I have planted. Perhaps what has given me almost the greatest pleasure of all is to discover the effect the garden can have on all sorts of people who come to visit it. For me, the joy is to share what I have created with others and to witness their reaction to each part of it. As I walk round the garden today I am full of gratitude to all those remarkable people who have helped me pull it all together.

I am particularly indebted to Paddy Whiteland, the irrepressibly unique Irishman who I inherited as part of the house and garden. Nothing was too difficult for him; he could spirit people and things out of thin air and he was the most loyal man I have ever come across. Mollie Salisbury and Miriam Rothschild were a crucial influence in those early days on my road to organic discovery and introduced me to another dimension of life for which I shall be forever grateful. Vernon Russell-Smith provided excellent advice on the Woodland Garden, while Rosemary Verey's brilliant plantswomanship has been of inestimable value in various parts of the garden. Sir Roy Strong brought his topiarizing skills to bear and the result has been stunning.

In writing this book with Candida Lycett Green, who, apart from having a wonderful eye for things of beauty and idiosyncratic character, has known my garden ever since I first set foot in it, there has been much pleasurable walking and talking about the garden.

Many talented people have been so kind in advising me and in helping to create some of the 'details' in my large canvas. Having said this, Highgrove is still very much my own garden, and so, I feel enormously fortunate to have had the opportunity, while in this life, to contribute to what I hope has been the enhancement of one small corner of this ancient land.

1 The Setting

THE GARDEN AT HIGHGROVE IS BRILLIANT. It shines. This is not just because it leads you through so many different moods and worlds and emotions, but because from its first beginnings in the early eighties it has been run on organic lines. Today this shows more than ever. Birds, bees and butterflies have proliferated, plants thrive in their organic compost and the vegetables are tasty, safe to eat and plentiful. Highgrove demonstrates the perfect miniature ecosystem. Everything feels right and as it should be. The Prince of Wales has made it crystal clear that it is better to work with Nature than against it. He may be an idealist, but by acting on intuition he has also become a visionary, with his gaze focused on future generations. It will take a century to restore the lost habitat of the Wild Flower Meadow and his newly planted trees will take

Right: *The eastward view from Highgrove's front door of the great eighteenth-century Gothic-revival church of St Mary's rising above the Cotswold roofs of Tetbury. Aberdeen Angus cattle graze in the foreground.*

Below: *The eastern front of Highgrove facing the park. North Country mules, along with black Hebridean sheep, keep the grass cropped. The Prince is Patron of the Rare Breeds Survival Trust.*

a century to mature, but his patience and good husbandry know no bounds. If the Prince could ever be said to wear his heart on his sleeve, it would be here at Highgrove.

Highgrove does not lie in the glamorous, deep-valleyed, tourist-trailed stretch of the Cotswolds, but in a gentle, unregarded side of Gloucestershire which the Prince loves. It is 'unobvious' England. Wide-verged lanes wind between dry-stone walls and flattish meadows, leading to buff-coloured villages like Shipton Moyne just beyond the rise, whose modest church harbours a startlingly beautiful monument. This is a landscape of hidden surprises.

Twenty years ago, when Highgrove was for sale and the Prince first drove up the drive, he fell in love with the *place*.

Left *and* **overleaf:** *The house from the south-east, showing Felix Kelly's adornments of pediment, urn-topped balustrade and pilasters to the plain house that the Prince bought. Ox-eye daisies and buttercups flood the front drive in early summer.*

Below: *The house was built between 1796 and 1798 for a local landowner, John Paul Paul. It was probably designed by the mason-architect Anthony Keck.*

Above: *In 1896 Highgrove was badly damaged by fire. Arthur Mitchell, the owner at the time, restored it in a lavish but slightly heavy-handed manner, adding a large north wing.*

Left: *Highgrove as the Prince first saw it in the early 1980s. The north kitchen wing had already been much reduced during the 1960s.*

It was the great cedar of Lebanon, the house, the stables close by, the soaring spire of Tetbury church seen across the park of ancient trees which made him feel happy here. There was a neglected walled garden of mellow red brick hidden beyond a copse, old pastureland and hollow oaks. The Prince saw the late eighteenth-century house – then ungainly and austere – and its dull garden as a wonderful opportunity.

The house had been built between 1796 and 1798 for a local landowner, John Paul Paul. It was probably designed by the mason-architect Anthony Keck. A century later High Grove, as it was then called, was badly damaged by fire and all the original interiors went up in smoke. In 1896 Arthur Mitchell restored the house in a lavish but heavy-handed manner, blunting its original elegance and rendering it stark and plain. The Macmillan family, who lived here immediately before the Prince, pulled down most of the large Victorian north wing, leaving only a portion which houses the kitchen. Today the latter structure is hidden by a tapestry of yew, holly, box and ivy, which has been allowed to grow in a wonderfully wavy and theatrical way to the roof line. The main block of the house has been reawakened through the artist Felix Kelly's lightening touches. His designs for the Prince replaced the solid stone parapet with an urn-topped balustrade, added a pediment and sharpened up the Ionic pilasters. The planting

Below: Aberdeen Angus graze in the lime avenue which was planted in 1995. The sun shines down its axis at midday.

which has now grown up directly around the house has softened its former gauntness and anchored it to the ground. It has a settled and right feeling.

The gentle curve of the front drive is lined with the lime trees that the Prince planted when he first came. In summer a coloured carpet of wild flowers spreads beneath them and away across a meadow to the west. Here ox-eye daisies and meadowsweet, yellow rattle, cowslips, poppies, corn cockle, cornflowers and corn marigolds all combine to create a startlingly beautiful first impression.

From the front door, the view across the park of the triumphant Gothic-revival church of St Mary's, rising above the jumbled limestone roofs of the market town of Tetbury, is as glorious as it was ever designed to be in 1893. Hamilton Yatman, then the owner of Highgrove, paid for the rebuilding of the church tower to the glory of God and as a memorial to his son, William. The work was undertaken 'on the understanding that he and his heirs and successors can continue an uninterrupted view from Highgrove'. There in the churchyard of St Mary's lies the nineteenth-century poet and novelist George John Whyte Melville whose immortal lines 'I freely admit that the best of my

Above: *Black Hebridean sheep graze peacefully in the park.*

Below: *Lime trees the Prince planted when he first came to Highgrove line the curve of the front drive.*

fun, I owe it to horse and to hound', live on into a third century, printed inside the cover of *Horse and Hound* each week.

In summer, horses rest in the wide shade of immemorial trees growing in Middle Park, which slopes gently away in front of the house. There are 200-year-old walnuts, common oaks and a 300-year-old hollow ash tree of which the Prince is particularly fond. He has planted young limes, walnuts, three cedars of Lebanon and many more trees in the fields around the house and in the Park where a flock of black Hebridean sheep graze incessantly. Aberdeen Angus cattle wander through the fields beyond, their cowbells (brought back to Highgrove from Switzerland and Italy by the Prince) ringing out different notes in a faintly heard cacophony.

The garden offers constant glimpses of the surrounding country – perhaps through a window cut into a yew hedge, or across the Wild Flower Meadow. There are few boundaries between the farm and the garden, they run in and out of each other. The garden is nourished by farm manure, while the crystal clear water in the field pond is the purified product of Highgrove 'manure'. The Prince proudly refers to his highly

Above: *The front drive to Highgrove in the early eighties showing an ancient Luccombe Oak on the left.*

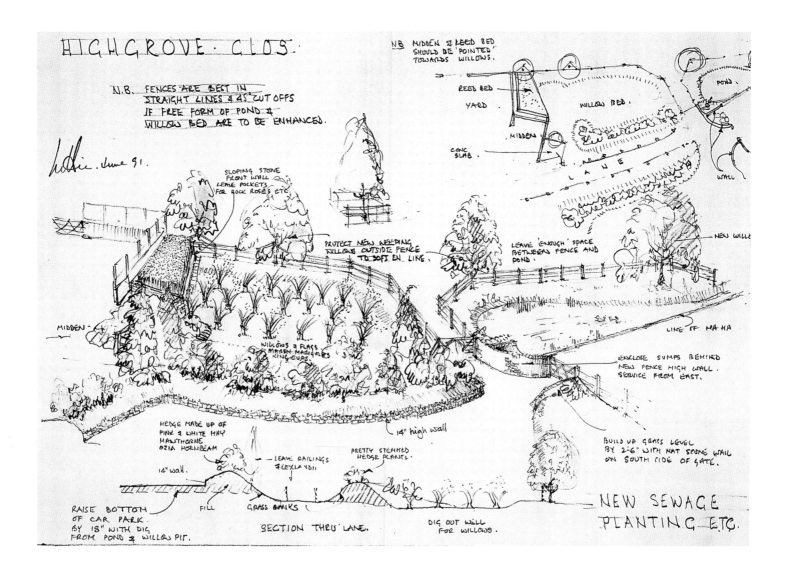

Above: *Drawing by architect William Bertram, responsible for the landscaping of the Prince's 'Sewage Garden'. It demonstrates the system by which the raw sewage is filtered through a bark-filled pit, reed and willow beds until it becomes a pond of clean water.*

successful system for processing raw sewage from the house as 'my Sewage Garden'. The sewage runs into a bark-filled pit, filters through reed beds, then through willow beds studded with marsh marigolds, and finally into a sump and out into a pond of clean water. In the early nineties the banks were planted up with a medley of water-loving plants, including sweet flag, water forget-me-nots, yellow flag, purple loosestrife, water mint, reed-mace, flowering rushes, lesser pond sedge and marsh marigolds, all species selected to attract dragonflies. Water plantain and white water lilies thrive in the area known as the 'swamp zone'. In the 'floating leaf emergent zone' there are amphibious bistort, yellow water lilies, arrowhead and purple iris. The 'pre-floating zone' contains frogbit, and the 'submerged zone' has spiked water milfoil, curled pondweed and fringed water lily. Almost as soon as the planting was complete, dragonflies began to breed and their larvae are to be

Above Right: *The back of the new beef shed designed for the Prince by William Bertram. A mixture of wild flowers grows in the foreground.*

Right: *Examples of baskets and plant frames for garden climbers made from Highgrove willow and sold in the Shop.*

found in the pond. The willows in the Sewage Garden are pollarded each year and the cuttings are used to make baskets for the Highgrove Shop. The simple and satisfactory sewage system inspired Una Black to write to the Prince after a visit to Highgrove in September 1998 with the Upper Thames Protection Society:

> We were particularly interested in the Reed Bed waste system which was very clearly demonstrated by David Howard, your enthusiastic and very helpful Head Gardener. For the sake of the River itself, we intend to try and encourage introduction of reed bed sewage systems in the Upper Thames Valley by acquainting local Councillors, Planners, Government Agencies, etc. with the idea at every suitable opportunity. Having seen the Highgrove system at work, we are now able to do this with much greater

Left: *Rare apples from the National Fruit Collection at Brogdale in Kent grow from a bed of Lavandula angustifolia. Beyond is the new beef shed built of chalk, brick and stone salvaged from a derelict building on a Duchy farm in Dorset.*

Above: *Part of a recently built dry-stone wall.*

Far Left: *Garden designers Julian and Isabel Bannerman were commissioned by the Prince to design something for the top of the existing column at the end of the lime avenue. Their galvanized and gilded steel* Column Bird, *rising from a nest of oak and palm leaves, was the result.*

Left: *Isabel Bannerman's sketch for the* Column Bird.

Below: *The cast-iron column on which the bird sits was rescued from the front of the old Victoria Station in London.*

authority. The recycling of reeds and willows, compost making and, of course, creation of new natural habitats for our sadly vanishing wildlife are very important additional benefits for us to broadcast too.

Striking away north-east from the front of the house, across Tanner's Park and towards Longfurlong Lane, the Prince has planted an avenue of limes nearly half a mile long. At the end of it there is a majestic column, which was saved from the demolition of Victoria Station in London and presented to the Prince, who asked designers Julian and Isabel Bannerman to create something to crown it. In April 1997 they wrote:

We walked out again to the column. It does look terrific. It is seriously big. We think anything to go atop o'it will have to be considerable, a heron on its nest about twice life size. We can see it made of sharp angular metal welded together...but gilded...the idea of the angularity and the 'flightfulness' we are after, the heron being on the point of landing.

The bird, a gigantic stork-cum-heron, looks spectacular alighting on its tangled nest of metal sticks to which oak and palm leaves have been welded.

From the west side of the house the view is directed on over the back drive and down another avenue of lime trees which march up the field known as Big Plummer. At the end is an eye-catcher in the form of a graceful dovecote designed by David Blissett, who sent his initial drawing to the Prince with this explanation:

> The materials of the dovecote are typically of the Cotswolds, with an emphasis on robustness and low maintenance. The roof is of Cotswold stone tiles laid to diminishing courses which could be made by reasonably local craftsmen such as those who worked on the new Cotswold stone roof at the Royal Agricultural College, Cirencester....The decision to form a peristyle or columns about the dovecote and extend the roof was taken so that a simple plain wood circular bench seat might be incorporated which would afford the opportunity of sitting at the dovecote and gazing at the landscape and animals round about.

The dovecote, a traditional element in any eighteenth-century landscape, has settled in and today it looks as though it has always been there. The doves get their water from the old carriage wash pond that lies beside the back drive to the

Below Left: *Designs by the architect David Blissett for the dovecote which stands at the end of a lime avenue. It creates an eye-catcher to complete the view from the garden side of the house.*

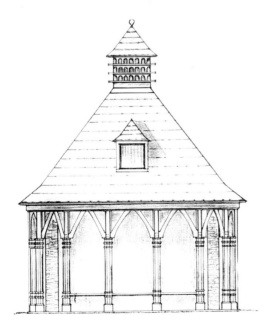
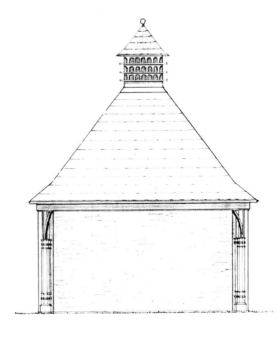

house. For many years the pond was filled in and it had become practically invisible. It was the Prince's idea to have the area excavated, restoring the pond to life.

Tudor Davies was a constable in the police post at Highgrove for nearly eight years. In addition to watching for terrorists, he was on nature alert. In June 1993 he wrote to the Prince:

My latest project is collecting the exuviae of dragon- and damsel-flies from the carriage wash pond and sending them to Mr McKenzie Dodds for positive identification. It will be interesting to see if numbers of species increase as the pond becomes more established. My latest news is a bit of a disaster, my pocket tape recorder which I use for the nest-box records and natural nesting sites has gone on the blink. Where I thought all my comments on the breeding season were safe and sound on tape it was not to be. When I

Above: The dovecote was built in the late eighties in memory of Sir John Higgs, a much-loved former Secretary of the Duchy of Cornwall.

Above: *The old carriage wash pond, which was filled in when the Prince first came. After having it excavated, he planted it up with flags, flowering rushes and many other plants designed to attract dragonflies.*

Far Right: *There is a continual police presence at Highgrove. Here a constable is seen bicycling up the front drive.*

came to write up the record cards there was absolute silence so unfortunately there will be no nest-box survey for 1993. Next year it will be back to the faithful pen and pencil and notepad. To hell with modern technology. I will keep you informed of any developments on the wildlife front as they occur.

Since then frogs, newts and toads have colonized the pond and a kingfisher was spotted by Tudor making a royal visit. Chiffchaffs, treecreepers, long-tailed tits, goldcrests, tawny and little owls are often seen and the garden is full of birdsong.

The Prince has made Highgrove into a perfect habitat for local wildlife. All over the Duchy farmland, both around the garden and beyond, he has created hedges and green lanes and planted copses near which migratory quails have been known to settle. A field called the Fourteen Acre, which lies along the road that leads towards Westonbirt, is lush with red clover and thick with butterflies on early summer evenings. New oak saplings grow apace and everywhere the signs of stewardship are exemplary. The Prince has always practised what he preaches. He set the wheels of organic farming and gardening in motion when he first came, although it would have been far easier not to. The ground elder on the garden paths and the docks in the fields would soon have shrivelled and died after a dose of poison and the flowers and the farm crops would have grown faster with the help of artificial fertilizer. The conservative Prince's Council, which is the 'Board' of the Duchy of Cornwall, of which Highgrove is part, would have been far happier too. They tried to dissuade the Prince from taking the organic route, but he was adamant. Now the farm is famous throughout the country and beyond. Duchy Originals biscuits made from wheat grown on the farm sell internationally and royalties benefit the Prince of Wales's Charitable Foundation.

Just over the perimeter wall of the Cottage Garden, beside the dragonfly-filled carriage wash pond, there is a new orchard of the rarest, most beautifully pruned and canker-free apple trees. Among them are 'First and Last', 'London Pearmain' and 'Devonshire Buckland', all presented to the Prince by the

Left: *Clumpy Tuscan columns support the loggia that runs along the front of the Orchard Room. The latter was built to allow the Prince to hold seminars, conferences, receptions, dinners, lunches and concerts, and to accommodate the thousands of guests and garden visitors that he entertains each year from the huge range of organizations he supports.*

Right: *The architect of the Orchard Room, the Norfolk surveyor Charles Morris, incorporated local styles and materials into the design.*

Brogdale Horticultural Trust. This is a charity which holds the national collections of apples and all other fruit trees. The trees are underplanted with various forms of *Lavandula angustifolia,* lavenders which have been specially selected for oil production. The plants were supplied by Norfolk Lavender Company and their blooms are harvested just before they open and sent to Norfolk for distillation. The scented oils are sold in the Highgrove Shop.

Charles Morris, the Norfolk surveyor, was the architect of the Orchard Room beyond the trees. It was built between 1997 and 1998 and designed to solve the problem of accommodating the thousands of guests that the Prince invites each year to dinners and receptions given for the many charities and organizations he supports. Highgrove House itself is not large and the new building has replaced the marquee that seemed to be a permanent feature in the park or garden. It is a beautiful essay in the Arts and Crafts tradition. Its clumpy Tuscan columns recall those of the old piggery building in the farmyard and also of the seventeenth-century market building in Tetbury. 'It is neither rustic nor classical', says Charles Morris, '...a country building of elegant robustness, but with an order imposed on it.' The varying shades of pale gold materials are local and most of

VIEW FROM D

Above: *A sketch by Charles Morris for the Orchard Room.*

the craftsmen who worked on it either live locally or come from Norfolk. The building has settled into the landscape, its gentle slope falling away to a copse on the edge of Tanner's Park. The Orchard Room is dedicated to the memory of Paddy Whiteland, who worked at Highgrove for nearly fifty years. He is depicted in a bas relief in the entrance hall which was carved by Nick Cuff, a sculptor from Tetbury who knew Paddy. It is a fine memorial to the great Irish character who was such a lifeline to the Prince during his first years here.

Nearer the house, large, golden Wellsummers and browny-black Maran chickens cluck and strut about in a little glade of trees and shrubs, a chicken's favourite sort of habitat. In its midst is one of the grandest chicken houses in the land. Cruciform in shape and tiled with little wooden shingles, it was designed by Richard Craven of Shropshire. The chicken run is

Left: *The Chicken House, where the Prince keeps Wellsummers and Marans, has a cedar shingle roof and was designed and built by Richard Craven. The galvanized steel cockerel on top was made by David Howarth.*

Right: *The Prince prunes the lower branches of a lime tree in the garden.*

Left: *The chickens are enclosed by a 'park pale' deer fence adapted for them by Richard Bower, who has made all the cleft oak and chestnut fencing and gates at Highgrove.*

enclosed by a 'park pale' deer fence of cleft oak. The pales are set at three heights, ranging from 3ft to 6ft. The Romans invented this design to enclose deer, as they will not jump a fence with a jagged outline. Richard Bower from Winterborne Zelston in Dorset adapted the deer fence to make it fox proof. One night a policeman observed on the closed-circuit cameras that there were no fewer than six foxes surrounding the pen. None of them attempted to scale it.

Nearby is the real heart of the matter, the compost heap. David Howard, Highgrove's Head Gardener, treats it as his altar, '...and you need to place all your faith in that altar' he says. Brought up in South Staffordshire, he began his working life as a garden boy at the local big house, Thorpe Hall, and went on to learn more about horticulture at the County College. He then joined a training scheme which made him an apprentice, first at the Savill Garden in Windsor Great Park and then at the Gardens of Windsor Castle. Although he was only seventeen at the time, he already knew that his life would be devoted to gardens. His apprenticeship over, he continued

Left: *David Howard,
the Head Gardener,
beside a compost heap at
Highgrove. Maintaining
the fertility of the soil is
the key to successful
organic gardening, and
compost is central to this
process.*

to learn more at the Royal Botanical Gardens in Edinburgh.
This was the moment of his great conversion. He happened
to see a tiny card in the window of an Edinburgh post office,
advertising the position of 'Garden Help'. He answered the
advertisement and later he was interviewed by Elizabeth
Murray who asked him if he had any references, 'Well, I
worked for the Queen at Windsor Castle,' he said. To this
she replied, 'That is all very well, but what do you know
about organic gardening?' It soon emerged that she was the
Regional Secretary for the Soil Association and it was from
her that he learnt about organic gardening. In addition to
his practical work, she made him read important books on
the subject, such as *The Silent Spring, Small is Beautiful* and
The Living Soil.

When David Howard came to Highgrove in 1997, the first
radical change that he made was to the management of the
compost heap. His fundamental rules are quite straightforward

Above: *Leaf mould stored
in the shade of a tree on
the side of the Park. Dead
leaves are never mixed
with the compost because
they contain tannins
and lignins.*

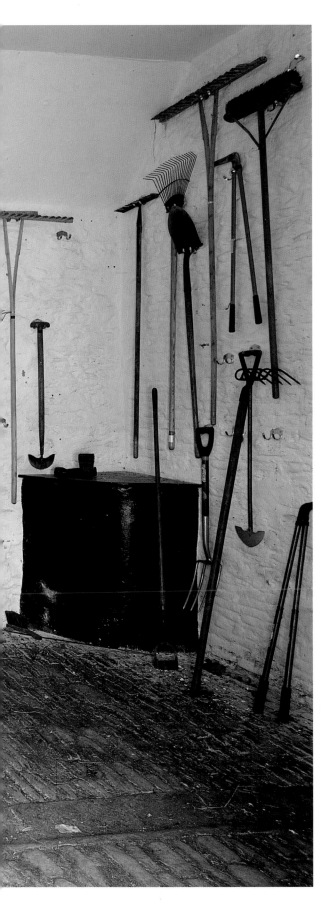

Left: *All of the tools are cleaned and oiled before they are put back into their allotted spaces in the tool shed.*

and his methods are scientific. For example, no dead leaves are put on the heap because they contain tannins and lignins. Fallen leaves form a separate pile which rots down into traditional leaf mould, a good source of humus that is low in nutrients. Woody material is also excluded as it takes far too long to rot down. Instead, it goes into the chipper and is turned into a mulch used to smother weeds. Nettles are welcome because of their exceptionally high nutrient content which helps to produce good compost. Grass clippings are mixed with waste straw to balance the carbon-nitrogen ratio and the heap is forked over at least once a week. When the bin is full it is covered with old carpet for twelve weeks. It is then brought under cover in a small section of the hay barn. Here it is stored until it is needed in the garden where, in time, it will enrich every living thing. Some underground irrigation has been removed in places where the compost is sufficiently thick. Once the worms get to work, moisture can be retained through a whole summer, however hot and dry it may be.

The tool shed is another of David's areas of hallowed ground. Plastic and metal handles have been banned from the gardens in favour of wood. Many of the tools have had their original handles removed. The new handles have been made by a craftsman who practises the art of making garden implements. All of the tools are perfectly balanced, to make a lighter job of heavy tasks. A well-balanced fork allows you to dig without straining your back, while a heavy and unbalanced one can wreak havoc on your body within minutes. Everything hanging on the whitewashed walls is gleaming. With steel blades well oiled, the tools are all set to do their level best in the garden.

2 The View from the House

T HE CALM OF THE GARDEN AT HIGHGROVE is a vital antidote to the Prince's public life. It is his haven, a loved and familiar place in which he can withdraw from the rest of the world. Perhaps this is so for any gardener who has a busy life, but Highgrove is no ordinary garden. For a start, there is a continual police presence. There may be a hidden camera in the tree you gaze at or a policeman using a mobile phone behind the next hedge. Secondly, since the late eighties, the Prince has allowed various interested groups to visit his garden – local charities, women's institutes, garden societies and so on. It started off as a small project, but now over 250 groups visit each year. In consequence, you are likely to bump into members of the

Right: *The view to the west through the french windows in the hall. The design for the fountain with the millstone at its centre was the combined effort of the Prince and the sculptor William Pye. It stands in the middle of the Terrace Garden and draws the eye up the Thyme Walk to the distant view of the dovecote.*

Left: *The west side of the house, enveloped by the garden and overhung by the towering cedar of Lebanon.*

Jerusalem Botanical Gardens Group, the Epsom Group of the Soil Association, BOG – the Birmingham Organic Gardeners – or the trustees of the Prague Heritage Fund. Thirdly, to thank the Prince for the myriad public duties he performs each year, he is given an inordinate number of presents. These range from whole collections of apple trees or ferns to statues, seats and other garden objects in every variation of style from all over the world. Many of these must be planted or placed for diplomatic reasons alone, giving the garden an eclectic and occasionally eccentric feel. Lastly, the Prince has been the recipient of an unprecedented amount of advice, from both well-meaning visitors and professional experts. Through this veritable jungle of 'Oh, you must plant this' or 'Why haven't you planted that?' he has managed to steer his own course. When Sir Simon Hornby, President of the Royal Horticultural Society, recently proffered advice on roses to plant to grow up apple trees: 'Blairi Number Two', 'Emily Gray', 'Long John Silver', 'Madame Caroline Testout', 'Gloire de Dijon', 'Zéphirine Drouhin', 'Rêve d'Or' and 'Pink Perpétué', the Prince instantly knew which he preferred. Twenty years ago the list would have meant nothing.

Above: *Tigga surveys the front drive from a favourite vantage point. Vitis coignetiae clambers up the house above roses, Senecio greyii and euphorbia.*

Right: *The Prince's love of terracotta pots is in evidence all through the garden. He arranges them himself as here, on steps leading to the Terrace.*

Left: *The west front of the house, taken when the Prince first came, showing the dull gravel path and the 'blobs' of golden yew.*

Below: *A door designed by William Bertram leads from the Terrace to the Sundial Garden which was the first garden to be created when the Prince arrived at Highgrove. A display of 'Spring Green' tulips grows in the pot beside it.*

When the Prince first arrived at Highgrove the garden was almost non-existent. There was a gravel path around the house, wide expanses of lawn and only the majestic cedar at the back to lift the heart. An avenue of golden yew 'blobs' planted by the Edwardian owners lined a gravel walk leading out westward from the house. 'I didn't know a thing in those days,' admits the Prince. 'I still don't know much, but if Lanning Roper hadn't died, the garden would have been his vision. I was going to ask him to do the whole thing. Then I was suddenly left with this blank canvas.' The Prince turned for advice to his friend Lady Salisbury. He had long admired the organic principles that she introduced at Cranborne in the 1950s. She was one of the country's fiercest proponents of farming without pesticides. By 1981, when the Prince asked for her help, she had already been gardening organically for thirty years and had developed two of the most legendary gardens in Britain, first at Cranborne in Dorset, and then at Hatfield House in Hertfordshire, the Cecil family's Jacobean palace. It was here that John Tradescant, head gardener to Robert Cecil, the first Earl of Salisbury, first made his mark in the early seventeenth century. Lady Salisbury

made a study of Tradescant when she took over Hatfield in the early 1970s. Her knowledge of gardening is unbounded.

'What joy to be planning a new garden, there is no pleasure like it (except hunting)!' Lady Salisbury wrote to the Prince on 1 December 1981, '...and you are going to have a blissful time.' Two weeks later, despite a heavy fall of snow, the Prince and Lady Salisbury set to work laying out the new garden. She had suggested enclosing the area that is now the Sundial Garden, to form a private, sheltered place where the Prince could get away from both the wind and the telephoto lenses of the press. '...it didn't even seem to matter having the snow and ice,' wrote Lady Salisbury on 15 December, 'somehow it can show the bones of a garden....it's much more fun not having the pros in but I just pray I won't make a bog. The great thing is to know what you like and want.'

Lady Salisbury would have liked the rectangular space allotted to the garden to be bigger, to reflect the scale of the house. This was impossible, however, due to security systems that were already in place. Nevertheless, it looks well today. The surrounding yew hedge, shielded at first with an

Below: *The north-west corner of the Sundial Garden showing the mature yew hedge which the Prince and Lady Salisbury planted in the winter of 1982.*

enclosure of hurdles and fed twice annually with well-rotted farm manure, grew apace, sometimes over a foot a year. Inside the rectangle the layout of the semi-formal garden, as English as could be, dictated itself. First came an apron of paving next to the house, where the Prince could breakfast in peace on sunny mornings. Next came the placing of a sundial – a wedding present from the late Duke of Beaufort, made by craftsmen on the Badminton Estate. This in turn dictated the shape of the stone circle that surrounds it and defined the four curved beds around it. The garden is intersected by grass paths. A path to the south leads out of the garden, drawing the eye

Above: The south front of Highgrove, which looks on to the Sundial Garden, is smothered in sweet-smelling climbers, such as wisteria, honeysuckle, jasmine and holboellia. The sundial was a wedding present from the late Duke of Beaufort.

Left: *The old planting, chosen by the Prince and Lady Salisbury, included a profusion of lavender, standard honeysuckle, clematis, old-fashioned scented roses, peonies, iris and perennial geraniums.*

Below: *The garden moves on. In 1999 the old planting was swept away, leaving only the architectural bones of the garden. Box borders designed by the Prince were planted and a set of iron gates replaced a collapsing wooden arch.*

Opposite: *The Sundial Garden, showing the enclosing effect of the yew hedge, planted to provide privacy and, most important, shelter from the stormy blast at 350ft in Gloucestershire. The garden chair,* The May Throne, *was a gift from Simon Borvill, who designed and made it.*

Left: *The new planting scheme is entirely black and white. In this, its first summer, the garden was full of black-leafed 'Bishop of Llandaff' dahlias (disbudded of their red flowers), black grasses, black-stemmed dogwood, black violas, white poppies and aquilegia. In the spring it will begin with snowdrops followed by black and white tulips.*

Overleaf: *'Queen of Night' tulips.*

across the meadow, towards the hidden Walled Garden and the distant view.

The Prince was adamant about wanting the flowerbeds filled with old-fashioned, scented plants as he believes scent to be of the utmost importance in a garden. 'I also wanted to supply something for all seasons', remembers Lady Salisbury. 'In the spring there would be polyanthus, pansies and dwarf iris, in summer it would be filled with roses and herbaceous plants. In this garden late summer planting was not such priority because the Prince is not much at Highgrove at that time of year.' She planted the edges of the beds with lavender and each corner is marked by clipped box.

By early summer the Sundial Garden was to be a tumbling frothy mass of everything nostalgic: honeysuckle, old roses and lavender. After Lady Salisbury had visited Highgrove in 1989 she wrote:

> I was thrilled to see that I couldn't look over the hedges in the south garden...everything in that little garden seems to have gone rather wild and seeded all over the place – the things I put in all those years ago – some rather over the top, like the lavender which could do with renewing – I think it could look much nicer with a new planting up...

Nearly ten years later, when most of the plants had passed their prime, David Howard persuaded the Prince to make radical changes. The old planting was dug up, lock, stock and barrel, except for the clipped box sentinels on the corners of the beds. Then a lot of compost was dug in and the irrigation system taken out. In the spring of 1999 a very different garden altogether was planted. It is entirely black and white, the ultimate contrast, and begins its show in February with double white snowdrops under the red-stemmed dogwood *Cornus alba* 'Kesselringii' and continues through until October. There are the black and white tulips 'Queen of Night', 'Black Parrot', 'White Dream' and 'White Tocoma'; the late-flowering, green-eyed white narcissi are out in May in the pots and in summer the beds are packed with white aquilegia, poppies, violas, black grasses, black-stemmed dogwood and black-leafed 'Bishop of Llandaff' dahlias disbudded of their red flowers, black hollyhocks and angelica. Tepees of violet willow (*Salix daphnoides*) and white willow (*Salix alba*) act as climbing frames for *Clematis cartmannii*. The planting is symmetrical at the corners and flows more freely within the beds.

When Lady Salisbury visited Highgrove in June 1999,

Left: *The Victorian front porch of Highgrove added after the fire of 1893. The crimson glory vine* (Vitis coignetiae) *clambers around it and the ivy 'Paddy's Pride' climbs up the side.* Senecio greyii *and rosemary spill out on to the gravel below.*

with a bus load of museum supporters from Hertfordshire, she was enchanted by the new planting of her original garden and wrote to the Prince, 'I wonder if you have *Anthriscus sylvestris* 'Ravenswing' and *Aquilegia* 'William Guinness' in your black and white garden? I could send you seed if not.' She would understand better than anyone that gardens are ever changing.

Against the walls of the house much of the Prince and Lady Salisbury's original planting of old favourites survives. Scent is the order of the day and wisteria, honeysuckle, jasmine and holboellia smother the walls. Lilies and thyme, cistus, wintersweet, *Viburnum* x *bodnantense*, Mexican orange blossom (*Choisya ternata* 'Aztec Pearl'), *Senecio greyii*, rosemary, *Viburnum fragrans*, old-fashioned village pinks, border carnations, curry plant (*Helichrysum angustifolium*), geraniums, tobacco plants, night-scented stocks, winter iris (*Iris unguicularis*), crocuses and tulips, all throw up scent through the open windows. Combined with euphorbia and hebe, the plants form a billowing skirt which softens the height of the house. The crimson glory vine (*Vitis coignetiae*), 'Mermaid' and 'Iceberg' roses and the ivy, 'Paddy's Pride', clamber up the front façade. A massive terracotta pot, which stands in the small circle of grass outside the front door, is filled with a topiary yew ball in the winter, followed in spring and summer by an ever-changing combination of bedding plants. On either side of the gate into the park are two clipped ilexes.

When the Sundial Garden was finished the natural progression was towards the west side of the house. By this time the Prince had got the bit between his teeth and could not wait to press on. He wanted to create a larger area near to the house where chairs could be set out in the summer. The Prince and Lady Salisbury devised the hard landscaping. Although at the very outset consideration was given to using cobbles from Chesil Beach in Dorset, after reflection penantstone was used with cobbles from elsewhere. It was laid by the local

stonemason, Fred Ind, for whom the Prince is always full
of praise:

> Ever since I came to Highgrove I have been particularly
> blessed to have the services of this wonderful craftsman,
> whose incomparable skill and ingenuity have been
> responsible for virtually every stone or brick path, every
> square inch of terrace and each stone wall. It is only when
> you find yourself making a garden that you realize how
> much labour and effort has to go into such features to
> provide the necessary framework to build on.

The low, gurgling fountain at the centre of the Terrace spreads
over a millstone and was designed by the Prince together with
the sculptor William Pye. The pool surrounding it is full of the
small stones that the Prince brings home from foreign shores.
William Bertram, the respected Bath architect, built the
pepper-pot pavilions which are placed at angles on the two far
corners of the Terrace, combining with the low surrounding
walls to provide a sense of enclosure. Quatrefoil windows
echoing those of the pavilions have been cut into the yew
hedges beyond. The tiles inside the pavilions, designed by the
Prince to reflect the flowers of the Mexican orange blossom
that grows on the Terrace, were executed by the American
architect Christopher Alexander.

By the time it came to planting the beds beside the Terrace,
the Prince had begun to leaf through books on gardening. He
has never done things by halves and was determined to learn
everything he could. The huge *Magnolia grandiflora* climbing
up the house and spreading out over the paving was already in
place. It has grown a lot since the Prince came to Highgrove and
it gives an immediate sense of protection. All of the other plants
were chosen by the Prince himself. Now that the shrubs and
roses are mature, and the gaps between the paving stones are
stuffed full of self-seeded lady's mantle, honesty, wild
strawberries and poppies, as well as lavender, peonies, alliums
and pinks, it is a glorious place to be. Mexican orange blossom,

*Right: Looking across
the Terrace to the two-
hundred-year-old cedar
of Lebanon and the
stables beyond – reasons
for the Prince falling in
love with Highgrove in
the first place.*

*Below: More examples
of the terracotta pots that
the Prince has collected
from all over the world.*

Left: *One of William Bertram's pepper–pot pavilions encloses the south-west corner of the Terrace. Different spring bedding arrangements fill the pots each year, including viola, narcissus, veronica, tulips. senecio and box.*

Below: *Narcissi and tulips in a pot on the Terrace.*

Left: *Primula, aquilegia and alchemilla cram the crevices on the Terrace through the spring, and choisya and olearia surround it.*

senecio, rosemary, rambling 'Sander's White' roses and *Rosa* 'Pearl Drift', with its blush of pink, form comforting blobs around the Terrace, and honeysuckle rampages everywhere. Tall cones of Portuguese laurel have been planted in large terracotta pots flanking the north and south entrances to the Terrace, completing the sense of enclosure. Terracotta pots proliferate. In spring they are packed with bulbs and in summer stuffed with tender perennials like *Helichrysum petiolare* 'Lime-light', artemisia, rhodochitons, ivy-leafed *Pelargonium* 'Tomcat' and Bacopa 'Snowflake' and the marguerite *Argyranthemum frutescens* 'Chelsea Girl'. There are also pots of hellebores and cerinthe. Tender plants such as daturas are brought out on to the Terrace in pots from the greenhouse. Either side of the steps which lead down from the central french windows of the house, the Prince planted two *Viburnum carlesii* 'Aurora', his favourite viburnum. He freely admits that his original planting plan was not wholly successful. 'Half the things died and half the flowers are too big or too small in the places where I put them.' In fact, the random effect has been extraordinarily successful. It all serves to form a tumbling, beautiful and completely informal garden and, as with most things that the Prince is involved with,

Above: *A bronze chicken, a fiftieth birthday gift to the Prince, pecks at the lichen on the low wall enclosing the Terrace.*

it never stands still. He will always want to add things and make improvements to existing planting.

From the house, the Prince can look out across the Terrace or into the wide splashes of shade under the cedar tree where there are bird feeders and a large bird table inspired by a design on a Chinese lacquer screen. Virginia Lyon, who visited Highgrove with members of the Weald and Downland Open Air Museum, wrote in May 1996, 'My own personal delight was to hear so many birds singing, especially the garden warbler and chiffchaff, and to see a great spotted woodpecker on the nuts under the great cedar tree.' Curving round and away from under the bow window is a raised acid bed made especially for azaleas and rhododen-drons which would not be happy in the alkaline soil of Highgrove. The Prince has always loved azaleas, particularly the scented varieties, as they remind him of happy days spent as a child in his grandmother's azalea-filled garden at Royal Lodge in Windsor Great Park. This collection, which includes the hybrid rhododendrons 'Blue Tit' and 'Yellow Hammer', was a wedding present from Edmund Rothschild of Exbury in Hampshire, whose rhododendron garden is perhaps the most famous in the country.

There used to be an open lawn in front of the Terrace and it

Right: *The french windows on the west side of the house in the early eighties, showing the bare gravel where the Terrace is now and the* Magnolia grandiflora *which must be over 100 years old.*

Below: *The raised acid bed with sweet-smelling azaleas and rhododendrons such as 'Blue Tit' and 'Yellow Hammer' were a wedding present from the famous Exbury Gardens in Hampshire.*

Left: *The cedar of Lebanon, heavy with snow, hangs over the beginning of the Thyme Walk. The architectural lines of this bit of the garden, laid out by the Prince with the help of Lady Salisbury, come into their own in winter.*

Above: *A yew, clipped into shape as part of Sir Roy Strong's grand topiary scheme.*

was the Prince's idea to enclose it. He wanted a double avenue of pleached hornbeams, like the pleached limes at Chatsworth, to give a background to the golden yew balls that grew as sentinels to either side of the central path. He then came up with the idea of enclosing the wide strips of lawn that lay behind the hornbeams with long lengths of yew hedge:

> Mollie [Lady Salisbury] and I tried to lay it out with tape measures. We should have got a surveyor. Nothing lined up and when Roy Strong came to shape the topiary at Rosemary Verey's suggestion, he had a fit.

In June 1989 Sir Roy Strong, who has created a complicated topiary garden of his own in Herefordshire on perfectly symmetrical lines, had written to the Prince, 'I wish that I could present you with a Repton Red Book but I hope that the contents of this box might excite you as to the possibilities and delights ahead in the hedges at Highgrove.' (He had sent his plans and photographs of possible ornaments.) 'It opens with rather a blow, that the original yew hedge was not correctly planted.' He also complained that the pleached hornbeam avenues, which were planted in elongated rectangles and relieved by gaps halfway up with square plantings, did not relate to the bays in the yew hedge:

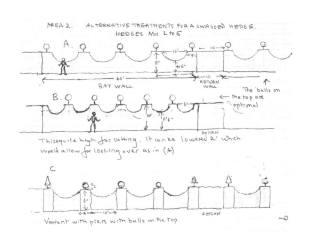

Thus great opportunities for grand vistas have been lost. How all this happened I do not know. Mollie Salisbury's hedge is out both sides by up to twenty feet on the right. …This has resulted in the curved hedges which act as curtain walls at the far end being uneven – one is about 135 feet and the other 160 feet. These problems need to be faced head on at this stage for they in fact condition the further development of that wonderful garden. Please do not be too downcast by all this and I feel sad that it has to be my melancholy task to point it all out! Much of gardening is 'fudging' up so that it looks reasonably right to the eye, and that is what I have attempted.…I have copied a set of designs for Rosemary Verey whose views I utterly respect.

It must have been like getting bad marks for an essay that you thought you had done so well at school. However, the Prince was undaunted and did not change any of the layout. With great panache, Sir Roy cut windows and bold swags into all the yew

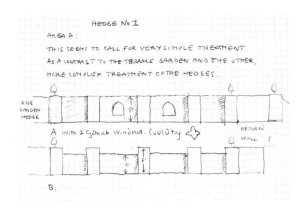

Above: *More designs by Sir Roy Strong for the yew hedges.*

Below: *The geometrical shapes of the yew hedges are clipped annually in August.*

Above *and* **Far Right:**
*The goddesses
representing the four
seasons, bought on the
advice of Sir Roy Strong,
came from Italy and
make a halfway break in
the long stretches of
pleached hornbeams.*

hedges, leaving critical stems which would eventually form lollipops. He used bamboos to mark the high sections and tied rope between them. The rope was heavy enough to fall into a perfect loop into which he cut. Sir Roy also suggested that the Prince should bring classical statues and stone seats from Italy, 'A few of these would give the garden a terrific lift in visual terms,' he wrote on 29 September 1989. The statues now stand among the hornbeams halfway up the avenue, where they withstand the odd battering by footballs kicked by the young Princes and their friends from what amount to two perfect small football pitches on either side of the avenue.

Finally, both Sir Roy and Rosemary Verey thought that the golden yews should be removed. In a letter to the Prince, Sir Roy said 'I think that once Your Royal Highness has taken the

Above: *The golden yews down the central Thyme Walk were just plain puddings when the Prince first came. Over the years they have been sculpted into eccentric shapes by the gardeners who were invited by the Prince to let their imaginations run loose.*

Left: *Weeding between the tapestry of thyme plants is a laborious task. There are more than twenty different sorts, which were all brought on from cuttings and were originally planted by the Prince.*

bold step of moving the acid yellow yews, you will realize how much the garden is improved by their absence?' The Prince took no notice. Today, the golden yew balls are triumphant. Lining the Thyme Walk – the central glory of the formal garden – they have never looked happier. Their golden leaves blend with those of the golden thymes in summer and in winter they turn a darker green. They are reminiscent of the great chessmen at Nancy Lancaster's famous garden of Hasley in Oxfordshire. The Prince asked his gardeners to clip the balls into 'eccentric shapes'. Art ran riot, and now each ball has a character all of its own which metamorphoses from year to year as new ideas spring up. This whole vista is entirely the Prince's inspiration.

By 1990 the Prince had grown tired of the rigid gravel path that stretched away into the distance. He decided to fill it in with random stone setts and paving, some from Broadfield, the

Above: *The Prince weeding the Fountain Garden where rosemary, achillea and perovskia complement the colours of the thyme with which it merges.*

Left: The bronze statue of a gladiator looks over the Fountain Garden and down the Thyme Walk to the west side of the house and the graceful cedar of Lebanon.

Duchy farm on the other side of Tetbury, some from Brackley and Avening. His plan was to grow thyme on either side. Fred Ind and Cecil Gardiner laid the path to the Prince's design; it was left unpointed and the gaps were filled with soil. Grit, sand and soil were then rotavated together on either side of the path to create a free-draining medium for the thyme to grow in. Meanwhile, hundreds of thyme cuttings were taken from stock plants belonging to Kevin and Susie White of Hexham Herbs in Northumberland and propagated in the Highgrove greenhouse. When everything was ready, the Prince began to plant the thyme plants himself. This was done between March and July 1990. From the tiny cuttings, great cushions of thyme have now spread out and crept into all the crevices and bare patches of the path. In summer when the thyme is flowering,

Above: One of the Italian statues which stands in a break in the rows of pleached hornbeams lining the Thyme Walk. The swagged yew hedge beyond encloses a spring display of bulbs and blossom.

Below: *These pots were shipped from Italy addressed to 'The Prince of Wales, Tetbury'. They were initially delivered to the local pub of that name.*

Right: *A detail of the paving in the Fountain Garden.*

the butterflies and bees abound. If the Prince has a large party, his guests alight on the drive and walk down the Thyme Walk towards the house. A thousand night-lights are set among the thyme and there could hardly be a lovelier sight or a more wonderful scent.

At the end of the Thyme Walk is the Fountain Garden. This was originally a raised, rectangular pool, breaking the flow of the vista from the house to the distant dovecote. The Prince asked William Bertram and William Pye to solve this problem by creating a new pool at a lower level. Bertram's pool is in the shape of a water-lily flower, which was the Prince's idea. It contains what Pye refers to as the 'pool within a pool with four waterfalls'. These waterfalls are created with four bronze water spouts which control the quiet and relaxing flow of water very precisely. In order to sit and look at it, William Bertram designed slightly raised seats on either side which are screened from the central vista by the golden yew balls. The yew hedge that used to enclose the old pool was moved to follow the shape of the new design and a planting plan for the beds around the seats was designed by the gardeners David Magson and James Aldridge. They followed a brief from the Prince who wanted to use rarer thymes here, unusual

Left: *The bronze gladiator is a copy of one at Houghton in Norfolk.*

Right: *Looking across the Fountain Garden to a raised platform where a seat designed by William Bertram mirrors the one opposite. White bearded irises in the foreground grow among rosemary, salvia and verbena.*

lavenders and rosemaries in a colour scheme that would link the area with the Thyme Walk. This aim was achieved by combining purple lavender, mauve perennial wallflowers, golden oregano, purple spires of Russian sage and silver artemisia, dark purple *Verbena bonariensis* and white bearded iris. The site, which is in full sun all day, is known as the Fountain Garden. Huge terracotta olive oil jars set formally at the four corners create a Mediterranean atmosphere. These jars were shipped from Italy in wooden packing cases addressed to 'The Prince of Wales, Tetbury'. Their arrival at Highgrove was delayed as the carriers initially delivered the cases to the pub of that name in the town. The gladiator that stands just beyond the Fountain Garden was given to the Prince by a friend. It is a copy of the one at Houghton in Norfolk, a place that the Prince has always loved deeply.

Left *and* **Right:**
Flowering cherries and daffodils make a spring display in the lawns that skirt the pleached hornbeams. An ancient oak towers above the yew hedge in the Wild Flower Meadow beyond.

3 The Cottage Garden

I**N SPRING AND SUMMER** the Cottage Garden billows with flowering shrubs, bulbs, roses and herbaceous plants. It is romantic to the hilt, small-scale, cosy, enclosed and shaded by walls and hedges, and its sinuous grass path leads you irresistibly on to discover hidden corners. When the Prince arrived at Highgrove this was a barren area, and yet it had a safe and settled feeling to it. Perhaps this was because it had always been the part of the garden most frequented by generations of Highgrove families: it was the nearest sheltered spot to the house and also a shortcut to the stables. Just past the cedar tree a door in the wall leads

Right: *Foxgloves have proliferated in the dappled shade of hidden corners of the Cottage Garden.*

Left: *A shower of apple blossom heralds an entrance to the Cottage Garden beside which a* Rosa rugosa *tumbles from behind a pot. The gate was designed by William Bertram and painted to the Prince's chosen colours.*

Left: *A door leading from the Pergola to the stable yard beyond.*

Below: *A little plaque of a tin mine let into the wall by the door is made from Cornish granite.*

Left: *The Pergola was designed by Charles Morris and built by Paul Duckett, Fred Ind and Steve Staines (who all work at Highgrove) in 1999. It replaces a wooden pergola which had rotted.*

Below: *Laocoön and his sons, the original of which is in the Vatican Museum in Rome, was sculpted by Andrian Melka, an Albanian studying in Dick Reid's workshop at York.*

into the cobbled stable yard which is filled with shining hunters throughout the winter. Farther along the garden wall, another door leads out to the cluster of farm buildings along the back drive, and the Orchard Room beyond.

From the Terrace, stepping stones in the grass wind past the raised acid bed to the ultimate Cotswold pergola. Its satisfactorily fat Cotswold-stone columns are shaped like enormous, elongated cotton reels which support the swooping shapes of the oak cross beams. This pergola has recently replaced an older, wooden structure which had rotted. It won't be long before it is showered with roses such as 'Madame Alfred Carrière', 'Zéphirine Drouhin', 'Veilchenblau', 'Bantry Bay' and 'Breath of Life', together with clematis, wisteria and honeysuckle. Much of the underplanting of the original pergola has survived, including pinks, violas, self-seeding love-in-the-mist, osteospermum and bearded irises. To either side are a series of yew shapes on raised grass mounds. These are gradually being clipped to form the Platonic Solids, representing the five basic elements of earth, fire, air, water and the heavens on one side, and the first five of the thirteen Archimedian Solids on the other. On the nearby wall, beneath the beginning of a yew

Left: *A bust of Leon Krier, the master architect of the Prince's Poundbury development in Dorset, surveys the new Box Garden. The bust was sculpted by Celia Maxwell–Scott.*

Right: *The newly planted Box Garden designed by the Prince. The winding paved path was laid out by the Prince. In time, the box will become a solid mass and will be clipped into billowing undulations.*

Far Right: *Stone plaques at the end of the Pergola commemorate the lives of former canine residents of Highgrove.*

arbour, is a stone relief of Laocoön and his sons. It was carved by Andrian Melka, a young Albanian sculptor who came on a Getty Scholarship from Butrint to study in Dick Reid's studio at York. He was already so skilled when he arrived that Reid could teach him nothing.

To the west of the Pergola lies the Box Garden, the latest in a long list of the Prince's original creations. Here a gargantuan terracotta pot is arranged to form the centrepiece, with a scattering of deep pink, carved sandstone from Hereford to the side. The arrangement will soon be frozen into a green sea of box, forming fossilized waves all around it. 'I got the idea of the box looking at a book on gardens in Spain,' said the Prince. A bust of Leon Krier, the master architect of the Prince's Poundbury development in Dorset, gazes over the garden. A serpentine stone path laid out to the Prince's design winds around what will be surging waves of green formed by various species of box planted in blocks. These will eventually grow to different heights, forming a series of solid undulations. The bulk

Below: *The swimming pool is partly sheltered by deep Cotswold tiled roofs covered in 'New Dawn' roses and ceanothus.*

Right: *A grass path winds like a small stream between luxuriant beds of herbaceous plants, including spiraea, hosta, salvia, monarda, hydrangea and stachys.*

of the planting is in *Buxus microphylla* 'Faulkner'. The higher blocks are formed from *B. sempervirens* 'Greenpeace' and 'Suffruticosa' and *B.* 'Green Gem'. The lower blocks are planted with *B. sempervirens* 'Memorial', *B. glomerata* var. *microphylla* 'Morris Midget' and *B. sinica* var. *insularis* 'Tide Hill'. There are also six pots of *B. sempervirens* 'Rotundifolia' which once stood in the Sundial Garden. The swimming pool is tucked into the back of an old Cotswold barn, its walls dripping with 'New Dawn' roses and ceanothus in summer. In time it will be screened by the yew hedges which are already half grown.

Through the first archway of fat stone columns, the Cottage Garden serpentines away towards a glade of laurels at its far end. Every so often there is a 'window' cut in the high yew hedge along the southern boundary, revealing vignettes of the wide lawns and the pleached hornbeam avenue beyond. Over the shrub-hidden wall to the north there are glimpses of farm buildings which look as though they have been there for ever. In fact, most of them were created from scratch by the Prince,

his architect William Bertram and the local builder David Palmer. The stone gable end of the beef shed pokes above the garden wall, its brick-edged embrasures and Cotswold tiled roofs covered in lichen and moss. A grass path meanders like a small stream between the loopy edges of beds banked up and stuffed to the hilt with cottage-garden flowers and shrubs, such as cistus, buddleja, mauve and white honesty, geranium, mock orange and gold-edged polyanthus, lungwort, campanula, aquilegia, weigela, the white 'Barnsley' mallow, cotton lavender, penstemon, salvia, delphiniums, lupins, and Michaelmas daisies. Among the more predictable plants are sudden surprises like the mahogany-red Cowichan primroses, *Cerinthe major* 'Purpurascens' or the spectacular, lemon-yellow flowers of *Paeonia mlokosewitschii*, 'Molly-the-witch', its botanical name derived from that of the Polish cavalry officer who discovered it. 'They gasp at that peony,' says Amanda Hornby, a voluntary garden guide, referring to the visitors she takes around the garden. 'They are all expecting something much more formal and flamboyant. They are generally amazed that it's not a grander garden, but one they can relate to, that's why it's so special.' Mrs Seema Kumar wrote, after she had visited the garden in the summer of 1995 with members of the Commonwealth Countries League, 'I found your home a "Home". Quite informal and with no

Right: *In a clearing, a wooden seat encloses a* Sorbus thibetica *'John Mitchell'. The seat was a present from the Prince's and Duchy of Cornwall staff for his fortieth birthday.*

Above: *Regal lilies flourish in lashings of Highgrove compost.*

Right: *The Cottage Garden in spring displaying tulips, narcissi and primulas.*

Left: *A collection of pots from different countries are arranged within a circle of laburnum trees. 'Ice Folly' daffodils grow in the foreground.*

Above: *Frances Baruch's bust of Laurens van der Post, the Prince's great friend and mentor, conveys a calm presence in the Cottage Garden.*

fancy show – some areas of your garden need watering but it was also reassuring to know that the hot weather has had problems even for you.' She went on to say that she thought the Highgrove Shop could do with a greater variety of tea towels!

Just inside the Cottage Garden there is a curved wooden seat, set back and surrounded by tumultuous roses. One of them, which has defied identification to date, grows in a sumptuous swag along a dipping chain over the low enclosing wall. In 1987, the plantsman Vernon Russell-Smith gave the Prince the roses 'Louise Odier', 'Souvenir de la Malmaison', 'Boule de Neige', 'Reine des Violettes' and 'Kathleen Harrop'. 'I thought they might all go into the beds either side of the seat where the Princess likes to sit…' he wrote. The grass path winds on between the beds, then widens out to a small lawn where a circular wooden seat, given to the Prince by his Office and Duchy staff for his fortieth birthday, is shaded by a *Sorbus thibetica* 'John Mitchell'. A bust of the late Laurens van der Post presides, exuding peace. There are big, biblical-looking terracotta pots lying under laburnum trees and an ancient *Clematis montana* winds like a boa constrictor up a huge hawthorn tree. Always, all through this wandering cottage garden, you feel happy. Was this because children had always played here?

In the 1950s, Lieutenant-Colonel Morgan Jones lived with

Above: *An unidentified rose smothers the chain it hangs along to form a swag above the three-sided garden seat, a wedding present to the Prince and Princess.*

his family at Highgrove. They were more interested in horses than gardens. Here though, on the north-west side of the house, they maintained a semicircular flower bed, a rockery and an Edwardian shrubbery. The children's Wendy house and sand-pit were here. The Morgan Jones employed the fabled Paddy Whiteland, a superb Irish horseman, as their factotum. He was still in post when the Prince took over thirty years later. Paddy's turn of phrase was legendary. 'A pig with one ear' was his description of this side of the garden after it was cut off from the lawns by the planting of the yew hedge along the Thyme Walk. The Prince agreed that the newly enclosed area 'now looked decidedly unprepossessing....After much reflection and contemplation I felt that the best solution for this awkwardly shaped area would be to try and create a cottage garden atmosphere.'

Below: *In spring the three-sided seat is surrounded by big clumps of alchemilla, 'Cottage' tulips and Narcissus 'Trevithian'.*

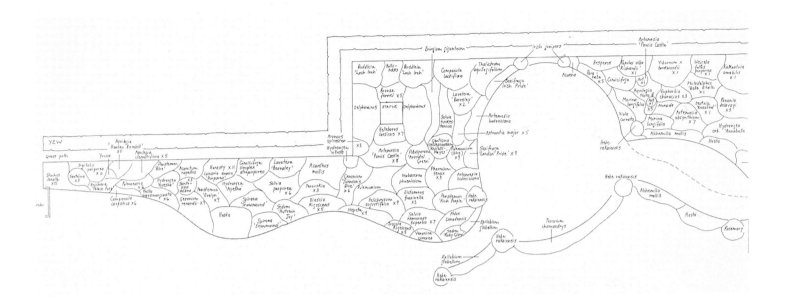

The Prince knew of Rosemary Verey's prowess as a plants-woman and had heard about her famous garden at Barnsley, not far from Highgrove. In the spring of 1988 he asked Rosemary to come and view the dismal area. It was defined by two wooden rose arches which the Prince had asked artist Felix Kelly to design (these were replaced by stone arches in 1999). The Prince was set on the idea of a winding path. 'We "walked" the path,' Rosemary remembers, 'and then drew it out on the ground with a flexible pipe and sand. It was to be wide enough for two people to walk comfortably abreast and the borders were to be edged with stone to allow the plants to flop over.' Once the borders had been generously fed with manure and the soil had settled, the planting could begin. Two vans full of plants arrived with Rosemary and, together with her friends John Hill and Rupert Golby, Trevor Jacobs, then head gardener, and the Prince, they worked all day. Prince William and Prince Harry lent a hand and Rosemary dictated the position of each plant. She has happy memories of the event:

The sun was shining, and for me – and I hope the others – it was a happy day. We had a picnic lunch on the terrace. We achieved a lot and when we were all exhausted and ninety per cent of the plants were in, we began to think about watering them. Just then an April shower began – a gentle one but just enough to revive the plants.

In the autumn of that year Rosemary ordered hundreds of bulbs. 'I'm glad that the *Garden in Winter* arrived,' she wrote

Above: Rosemary Verey's plan for part of the original Cottage Garden.

Below: Aquiligea 'William Guinness' syn. Magpie.

Right: *In high summer the flowers in the Cottage Garden spill over the grass path winding through it. Here white valerian,* Rosa *'Gertrude Jekyll' and campanula grow in and out of each other.*

Above: *Gilly Hayward dead-heads the large 'Marguerite Hilling' rose (the pink sport of 'Nevada') in the Cottage Garden.*

in December 1988. 'I went over to Highgrove on 26 November and put in quite a lot of bulbs so there should be interest there starting with crocus and early narcissus through to the tulips. I just hope that you will be there to enjoy some of them. They are a present to you.' The tulips included 'Angélique', 'White Dream', 'Black Parrot' and *kaufmanniana*.

Winding on through the last arch of the Cottage Garden, you come in to a clearing where a soft, billowing doughnut of box encircles a magical ilex. This is now called the New Cottage Garden and it was developed by the Prince himself in the early 1990s. Again, Rosemary Verey was involved with the planting, which was designed to provide interest throughout the year, 'hellebores were included for both winter and spring and also *Ligustrum japonicum* 'Rotundifolium' [Japanese privet] to confound the experts.' Viburnum, Mexican orange blossom, lilac and osmanthus were used as a background. In March 1992 Rosemary Verey wrote to the Prince, 'I hope you enjoyed and appreciated the hellebores I brought over on Sunday the

Above: *The intricate petals of* Rosa *'Gertrude Jekyll'.*

Right: *A Chinese Chippendale seat stands in the Cottage Garden.*

Right: *A cobbled path leads through the Laurel Tunnel past hostas and ferns to a 'Capitol Seat' made from pieces found in a reclamation yard by garden designers Julian and Isabel Bannerman.*

23rd. There were some very special ones, bought from Mrs Ballard, and other white ones from Barnsley.'

The perimeter wall shielding the garden from the back drive was built up in the 1980s and the bed below banked up so that the shrubs and small trees would provide immediate protection from the farm traffic. Known as the Savill Garden, it began to take shape in 1987 under the guidance of Vernon Russell-Smith, originally introduced to the Prince by Felix Kelly. Vernon Russell-Smith had already advised the Prince on much of the early and extremely valuable background planting at Highgrove and had curbed some of his hastier decisions in the early days of innocence. He managed, for example, politely to dissuade him from planting a hedge of Leyland cypress beyond the Walled Garden by telling him that the roots would be far too greedy to allow anything else to grow. For Highgrove's Savill Garden, viburnum, lonicera and eucryphia were obtained from the real Savill Garden at Windsor, together with silk-tassel bush (*Garrya elliptica*), cotoneaster and mock orange. The Prince has added to it with Rosemary Verey's help, and also planted presents from friends like crab apple trees and a beautiful *Magnolia stellata*. He now plans to enlarge the perimeter bed by extending it into the lawn to give a greater sense of secrecy.

In November 1996 Rosemary Verey was awarded an OBE for her services to the gardening world. Coincidentally, the Prince held the investiture. 'I loved every moment of the ceremony and the surroundings', Rosemary wrote to the Prince on

7 November 1996. 'How you can keep up your smile and your interest for one and a half hours amazes me…it makes me even more aware of how necessary it is for you to have time at Highgrove and behave like us ordinary garden owners…'

Beyond the Cottage and the Savill Gardens comes a sudden change of mood. Here, where once there was an impenetrable grove of laurels, the Prince has carved out a winding tunnel. In 1995 Julian and Isabel Bannerman suggested laying cobble-stones as the groups of visitors were turning the path beneath the laurels into a mud bath. They also suggested a site for a 'capitol seat' made from Doric capitols which they had found in a reclamation yard. 'The seat would look most handsome with ferns planted about it. *Dryopteris filix-mas* and *Matteuccia struthiopteris* which we always think of as the Prince of Wales' feathers fern,' they wrote on May Day 1995. Beside the path and in among the ferns the Prince has laid stone carvings

Above: One of the stone garden seats which Sir Roy Strong encouraged the Prince to buy in Italy. It is set in a more formal area behind the Thyme Walk and can be seen from the Cottage Garden.

Right: *The topiarized yew hedge provides glimpses of other parts of the gardens, this time through to the Wild Flower Meadow.*

Overleaf: *During the summer months, the Cottage Garden beds are an enclosing and intimate mass of herbaceous plants, roses and flowering shrubs.*

Right: *The beautiful blossom of a double white cherry seen against a blue, spring sky.*

Above: *A sample work by a student from the Prince's Foundation lies in the Laurel Tunnel.*

by students from the Prince's Foundation. This bit of the garden is the Prince's own and he tends to the invasive laurels himself. He always says he 'hacks' at things, but in fact he cuts the branches carefully when he thinks light needs letting in.

'I think about the garden a lot of the time,' says the Prince, 'I'm always having new ideas – I have dreams about the garden. Things do come from different dimensions, it's inadvertent.' If the Prince's ideas are intuitive, then the fact that they are carried through comes from a fierce desire to win and to be the best. He is nothing if not competitive. Paradoxically, he is diffident about accepting praise, but perhaps now that so many strangers are visiting his garden and expressing their appreciation, he may one day believe that he has succeeded. Jenny Scott, the Warden of the local retirement home, wrote in 1994 when she brought a group to Highgrove that included:

…one lady of ninety years who walked all the way around. It gave them all a great deal of pleasure, as some of the residents had worked in the house years ago, one gentleman had been the gardener for the Macmillan family, and another resident's father had been a gardener at Highgrove.…Personally, please may I thank His Royal Highness for the visit, to see the joy and pleasure on the faces of the residents as we made our way around the gardens…was really wonderful.

4 Wild Flower Meadow and Woodland Garden

ELEGANT WROUGHT-IRON GATES at the southern end of the Sundial Garden lead into the ravishing Wild Flower Meadow that lies to the west of the drive. In spring, these wide, open stretches of level grassland are sprinkled with a kaleidoscope of colour to beat the carpet of flowers in Botticelli's *Primavera*. This is Highgrove's crowning glory. By mid-April there are fritillaries, crocuses, cowslips, daffodils and the first buttercups spreading to east and west beyond the ancient oaks and chestnuts, until they merge seamlessly with the fields beyond and the parkland in front of the house. Great swathes of white and yellow daffodils provide blocks of colour on the outer edges of the Meadow and bound the trees. Cutting through the

Right: *The Bannermans' green oak temple in the Woodland Garden is glimpsed from the Wild Flower Meadow across a clump of daffodils.*

Left: *Many of the daffodils were already here when the Prince came to Highgrove. He has added clumps of white ones among them to give a mixed effect.*

Left: *Looking from under an ancient burred oak towards the south-west corner of the house across the Wild Flower Meadow in spring.*

Below: *The same view in the early eighties, showing the area that is now the Wild Flower Meadow.*

97

Meadow and linking the Sundial Garden to the Walled Garden is the Tulip Walk. It comes into its own in May. A mown grass path runs between a formal avenue of fastigiate hornbeams (*Carpinus betulus* 'Fastigiata'). To either side of it flow great purple rivers of tulips formed by 'Attila', 'Negrita', 'Queen of Night', 'The Prince' and 'Burgundy Lace'. Occasional clumps of 'The Bishop' create splashes of scarlet, a scheme inspired by the royal racing colours. Then the camassias, which seem to thrive on this poor Cotswold brash, begin to creep out into the Meadow in wide drifts of pale blue or the deep bluey-purple spires of *Camassia leichtlinii caerulea*, the Prince's favourite.

By early summer the whole area has become a hay meadow that Birkett Foster might have painted – the meadow of some

Left: The south side of the house and the enclosed Sundial Garden seen from the bottom of the Tulip Walk in spring. Fastigiate hornbeams form an avenue. 'Burgundy Lace', 'The Bishop', 'Negrita', 'Attila' and 'The Prince' tulips create a purple and scarlet swathe that represents the Royal racing colours.

Right: The gates leading from the Sundial Garden to the Tulip Walk were found in a reclamation yard by Julian and Isabel Bannerman and remodelled by Bob Hobbs. The Prince of Wales' feathers were wrought by Alan Cooper.

Left: The south façade of Highgrove in the early eighties, showing what was then a horse paddock in front of it.

99

Left: *Looking across the Wild Flower Meadow to the park. In spring the Meadow is full of buttercups, cowslips, dandelions and camassias.*

Above *and* **Right:** *Camassias with their elegant spires of star-shaped flowers; the Prince's particular favourite is the deep bluey-purple* Camassia leichtlinii caerulea.

distant memory where flowers proliferate among the different grasses until the hay is made in July. This is England, every bit of it. It is a picture that the Prince wanted to protect. The garden is not just a reflection of his personal taste but also of his extraordinary foresight and his determination to demonstrate what he believes is ecologically right for the world. So often he has been found to be years ahead of his time. Perhaps he does get fed with more information than most of us, but he disseminates it intelligently and acts on his own gut feelings. Since the Second World War, ninety-five percent of the country's herb-rich grassland has disappeared through modern farming methods. Far more silage is made than hay, leaving no seed, the 'weeds' are filtered out of the seed used for planting new grassland, and out of all cereal crops. More often than not, the native species growing along the edges of fields are poisoned by chemical drift during the spraying of the main crop, and roadside verges are frequently cut before the wild flowers have seeded. As a result, our native flora and fauna is diminishing at an alarming rate.

When the Prince first expressed his desire to conserve England's wild flowers and restore the natural habitat that had been destroyed by previous farming methods, it was Lady Salisbury who insisted that he meet Miriam Rothschild, one of the great women of the twentieth century. A fellow of the Royal

Above: *The Wild Flower Meadow in summer, looking towards Sir Roy Strong's scooped yew hedge, which encloses the formal gardens.*

Right: *Miriam Rothchild's 'Farmer's Nightmare' wild flower mixture seen here growing by the front drive. Yellow rattle, poppy, cornflower, corn cockle and corn marigolds grow among tall grasses.*

Society, she has written over 300 scientific papers and is the world's expert on fleas. She is also one of the country's leading proponents of biodiversity. In 1982, the Prince went to meet her on her estate of Ashton Wold in Northamptonshire, where she had given over huge walled gardens and greenhouses to the production of wild flower seed.

What Miriam Rothschild began at Highgrove was a genuine experiment. Until then no one but herself had planted wild flower seed directly into existing sward. The seed she used was harvested from a field of her own, but she had chosen wild flowers and grasses that would be typical of a Gloucestershire meadow, 120 different sorts, including hawks-beards, fescues, bedstraws, hawkbits, meadow vetchlings, trefoils, clovers, chickweeds, knapweed, cowslip and hairy violet. 'But will they grow at Highgrove?' Miriam wrote to the Prince in November 1982. 'We really won't know until the spring. In fact I'm extremely grateful to be able to try it out somewhere besides here. I am thrilled by the prospect of wild flower propagation at Highgrove, it is such a lovely spot and everyone will follow your lead!' She had included pyramidal orchids in the 'Highgrove Mixture', as she called it. 'The seed is as fine as lady's face powder…you never find it in the seed analysis. It just needs falling on the right habitat.'

At first the wild flower results were disappointing, perhaps because of a dense growth of dandelions over the entire field, and few of the species flowered. The grass called Yorkshire fog took over, but gradually, as the fertility level dropped, the flowers began to come back. There are thirty-two different species to date. In 1999 they included common spotted orchid, yarrow, agrimony, lady's bedstraw, meadow crane's bill, ragged robin, sainfoin, cowslip, self-heal, salad burnett, great burnett, red and white campion, red betony, devil's bit scabious, ox-eye daisies, buttercups and yellow rattle in abundance. It will take a hundred years to recreate the true, flower-rich meadowland of the past and the Wiltshire Wildlife Trust has been monitoring progress and helping with the restoration of the meadow over the last few years. Many of the recent successes have been the

Above: *Dandelion clocks in the Wild Flower Meadow.*

Left: *The 'Farmer's Nightmare' mixture on the east side of the drive includes poppies and ox-eye daisies. Newly mown hay lies in the park beyond.*

result of planting the flowers as plugs, and in 2000 some of the Hebridean sheep will graze the Meadow and help to open up the sward for seeds to germinate more easily. Perhaps beautiful Marsh Fritillary butterflies will soon be settling on the scabious. Certainly there are Small Blues, Green Hair Streaks, Speckled Woods and Meadow Browns. Rare bumblebees make nests in tussocks of the grass. Miriam Rothschild gave the Prince a collection of alliums to plant in the Meadow to give a good spread over the summer, but so far they have been reluctant to seed themselves. 'I am conscious that Your Royal Highness' interest in wild flowers at Highgrove has been of *vital importance* in…the campaign for protecting the wild flowers of this country,' she wrote.

The mixture of wild flower annuals she provided, sown in rotavated strips on either side of the front drive, is called 'Farmer's Nightmare' and produces a summer rainbow of poppies, pink corn cockle, cornflower and corn marigold

Below: *Seed for the original Wild Flower Meadow was specially formulated for Highgrove by the legendary proponent of biodiversity, Miriam Rothschild, to whom the Prince first turned for advice. She described the orchid seed as almost invisible, 'like lady's face powder'.*

Above: In 1999 the Wild Flower Meadow was mown in July. Here, the Prince is seen helping Jonathon Waterer with the job.

among the barley and oats. Cut down in July, the seed is then spread for the following year. This method of growing the cornfield annuals will soon be moved to a field behind the Orchard Room, as the shade from the curving avenue of limes which frame the flowering rainbow has grown too wide. The beech hedge along the edge of the park was planted more recently, despite Vernon Russell-Smith begging the Prince to resist. 'Let me be totally frank, Sir, no!' he wrote. 'I think you'd regret a beech hedge up the drive…it would shut away the feeling of the house being in a park…the wild flower planting would have the feeling of being in a bed…' He recommended park railing instead. But the Prince wanted a hedge and so he planted one.

While the flora and fauna at Highgrove are busy proliferating, so are the 'experts' who beg to visit. Neil Diboll, a landscaping consultant from the Prairie Nursery in Westfield, Virginia,

offered his advice to the Prince about the Meadow in an eight-page letter. He even suggested taking down the trees, to which the Prince replied:

> I'm afraid I like my trees in the meadow area – I have the national beech collection and quite a few of them are in the meadow. I fear it is too late now to start clearing the whole area and using Roundup on all vegetation. Apart from anything else, they are now finding rare beetles, invertebrates and wild bees in the meadow and I couldn't possibly do anything to them!

Among the insect species recorded in the Wild Flower Meadow are Welsh chafer (*Hoplia philanthus*) and the soldier beetle (*Cantharis lateralis*).

In the windless lee of the Walled Garden's north wall there is a small triangle of protected ground which is slowly being transformed into Highgrove's Southern Hemisphere Garden. The Prince is particularly fond of ferns and is keen to build up an important collection from the 600 or so varieties. Rare tree

Left: *An urn from Sri Lanka stands in the Woodland Garden where once there was a tangle of brambles, nettles and young saplings.*

Right: *Delicate tree ferns, a gift from members of the British Pteridological Society of which the Prince is President, stand in the windless lee of the Walled Garden.*

Left: *The fern* Dicksonia antarctica.

Right *and* Below: *One of the Spanish chestnut trees which stands in what was once the park surrounding Highgrove and is now the Wild Flower Meadow. The bark forms a spiral around the tree.*

ferns given to him in April 1999 by members of the British Pteridological Society, of which he is President, have been planted here. Inspired by the Logan Botanical Gardens on Scotland's Gulf Stream, this tiny corner of Gloucestershire will soon look even more exotic when the giant-leafed gunnera is growing from the deep, waterlogged ditch on the edge of the garden.

Above the gunnera-filled ditch is an old laurel shelter belt which edges the Meadow and leads towards the Woodland Garden. From here there is a fine view of the theatrical length of yew hedge with the Gothic windows cut through it. The hedge encloses the formal gardens with swooping swags. If you are exceptionally lucky, you might see a lesser spotted woodpecker on one of the stag-headed oaks that are the final vestiges of the eighteenth-century park. Around the trunks of some of the trees the Prince has planted blocks of box which form solid architectural bases. This idea was inspired by a visit to the gardens of Kyoto, where he particularly loved the way that the Japanese clip both evergreen and deciduous trees. There have been new plantings in the Meadow. During the eighties, for example, a Babylonian willow from the Chinese Academy of Forestry in Peking came to the garden via the Westonbirt Arboretum.

In the shadow of the Kitchen Garden wall, a small winding walk leads you into the woodland's dappled shade, where once there was a tangle of brambles, nettles, ivy and snowberry under a scattering of sycamores. It was a windy and forlorn spot which the Prince began to tackle in the late 1980s and has transformed into a series of wonderments. Up in the boughs of an old holly is a tree house built for the children by William Bertram. There was concern about the young Princes' safety at such a height and the Prince suggested a net of the sort that one might find under a trapeze artist at a circus, but this proved impractical. 'For my part, I have had a chance to think about how best the Princes should approach the tree house,' William Bertram wrote in June 1988. 'I don't think my original idea of a pole with broomstick handles is safe enough. I enclose a drawing showing a rather novel design for a rustic staircase up to the platform.' An elaborate stairway was built, up which thornless roses were designed to climb. The dark green balusters were to represent holly leaves and the red rail, berries. The door of the house is shaped like a holly leaf.

A little farther on, in a small clearing, is the most astounding

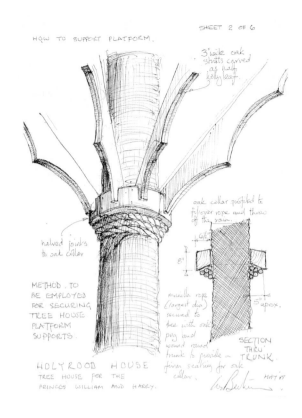

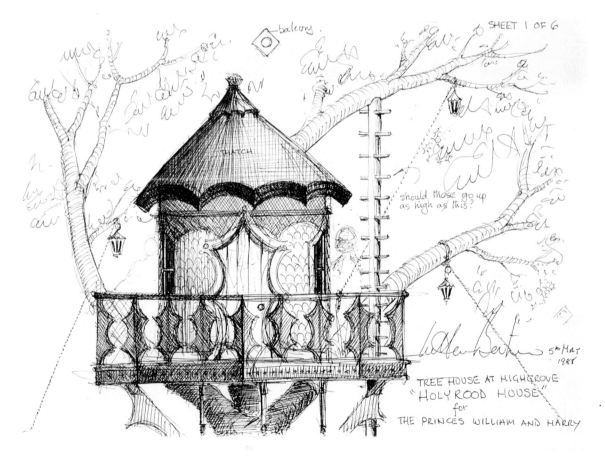

Above: *A detail of the exterior of William Bertram's tree house built for the young Princes, William and Harry.*

Left: *The original idea of a pole with broomstick handles up which to approach the house was abandoned in favour of a ladder.*

Right Above *and* **Below:** *More details of 'Hollyrood House'.*

Far Right: *The house was built in the boughs of an old holly tree in 1988 and echoes the holly-leaf design throughout. The leaf shapes of the balcony are painted dark green with rails of scarlet to represent holly berries dotted here and there.*

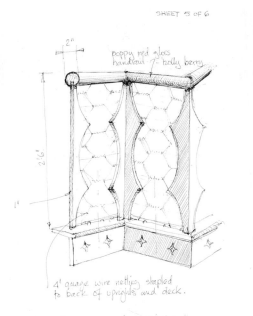

2"

poppy red gloss
handrail ∴ holly berries

2'6"

1"

4" gauge wire netting stapled
to back of uprights and deck.

Holly leaf balcony front - painted holly green.

HOLYROOD HOUSE   TREE HOUSE AT HIGHGROVE
                  FOR THE
                  PRINCES WILLIAM AND HARRY

Walter Barker '88

top secured to bough of tree

6'-4" stripped pole
with broom stick steps drilled through
turned 30" top 3 handles

1'-3" cut to choice
by H.R.H. P.O.W.

W   W

door

1'-6"   1'-3"

50"

90°

PLAN OF GALLERY

HOLYROOD HOUSE
FOR THE PRINCES
WILLIAM AND HARRY

A B C & D rungs to be
removable for ∴ by security.

A   9"   D.
           9"
B   9"
           9"
C   9"
           9"
D   9"

mild steel 3/8"
coach bolt
dropped into
hole.

1'-9"

2'-0"

stainless steel
pin in concrete
foundation
1'-6" sq. 9" deep

Right: *The 10ft-high fern pyramid designed by the Bannermans, under construction.*

Below: *After it had been filled with rich Highgrove compost, hundreds of hardy ferns, predominantly hart's-tongue, were planted through the mesh.*

Opposite: *William Bertram's gate in the boundary wall of the Woodland Garden.*

pyramid, covered in a solid mass of hart's-tongue ferns and moss. In autumn, when the woodland floor is covered in dead leaves, this sudden beacon of bright, shiny green knocks you for six. The Victorians may have dreamt up such an artistic extravaganza, but only Julian and Isabel Bannerman could have thought of building it today. They made a frame 10ft high from rigid wire mesh and filled it with Highgrove compost. The compost retains moisture, and the ferns stuffed into it have thrived. Various paths wander on, in and out of island beds among the trees. These are edged with split logs in which the Prince and Rosemary Verey have planted big blocks of foxgloves, *Campanula persicifolia*, hostas and Martagon lilies. A giant hogweed that they planted together grew to 14ft in 1999. Behind them and all around the outer edge of the Woodland Garden they planted large groups of shrubs – *Viburnum carlesii* and *V. tinus*, lilac and variegated hollies, box and variegated privet to buffer the piercing east wind. In spring, carpets of snowdrops, bluebells, whitebells, scillas, grape hyacinths and chionodoxas spread away in great pools and out into the light of the Meadow.

Among the shrubs on the outer edge of the wood is the Wall of Gifts, looking like the remains of some ruined cathedral cobbled together into vertical crazy paving. It is built largely from the left-over samples of work by students on masonry courses. When word got out that the Prince had found a use

for these stones, students began to send him samples and things that had gone wrong. The Wall also became a resting place for various stone gifts, such as the rampant lion from the Villa d'Este in Italy. The result could be the corner of the garden at a bishop's palace. The eclectic tapestry of stone can be continued whenever suitable carvings are collected. Julian Bannerman, whose inspiration the Wall was, did a rough

sketch for the builder to follow, 'My drawing looks like the
Beano,' he complained. Fred Ind, who has worked at Highgrove
for over twenty years, was bemused by it. 'It was quite an odd
thing to make for the likes of me. It looked very strange on the
paper. We wanted to make a good job of it but Mr Bannerman
wanted it all untidy.' In his artistry, Fred Ind, helped by Paul
Duckett, turned the wall into a minor masterpiece.

Above: *The Bannerman-
inspired Wall of Gifts was
made by Fred Ind and
Paul Duckett from bits of
masonry students' sample
work. It also includes
various stone gifts given
to the Prince.*

Above: Helleborus orientalis *hybrids thrive in the dappled shade of the Stumpery.*

Hidden until you stumble upon it is the star of the show, the moody, melancholy, mysterious and magical Stumpery. From the grave of the old acid bed of rhododendrons and azaleas, the Bannermans have created a completely secret enclosure. Two temples, built from green oak cut in to massive pieces as though it were stone, face each other across a grass circle dominated by a great oak tree, looking like the first beginnings of Greek architecture in some silvan glade. Curvaceous ramparts in a wild tangle of fern and hellebore-studded tree stumps enclose the glade. At the foot of the oak sits the *Goddess of the Woods*, especially commissioned for the Woodland Garden by the Prince in 1991 and made by the sculptor David Wynne, who returns from time to time to wax her. If you run your hand down her back you can feel each vertebra.

The semi-shade of the Woodland Garden provided an ideal setting for the creation of a Stumpery – a vestige of England's eighteenth-century Picturesque period. Tons of old roots and

Right: *A sweet chestnut stump archway was constructed by the Bannermans by stacking the roots like jacks. Convenient peaty pockets are provided for ferns and euphorbia.*

stumps arrived on an articulated lorry and were dumped by the side of the Woodland Garden. They looked like a huge pile of bones, although the gigantic sweet chestnut roots from Cowdray Park in Sussex resembled giant wisdom teeth extractions. The Bannermans wove and locked them together in fantastic contortions shaped into arches and waves around the temples. Paths of ammonites were laid. The pediments of the temples were filled with smaller bits of twisted wood that look like interlocked antlers, and roots were laid to line the edges of beds and paths. While the Bannermans were in the early stages of building the arches and ramparts, the Duke of Edinburgh walked around the garden with the Prince. On reaching the Stumpery he turned to the Prince and said, tongue in cheek, 'When are you going to set fire to this lot?'

An absence during April 1996 meant that the Prince was out of touch with events in the woodland area. A note written by the Bannermans to await his return read: 'Don't be too alarmed by what you find in the woods – it is completely naked and not

Left: *The architectural forms of the ferns and the euphorbia 'Mrs Rob's Bonnet', a form of wood spurge, and* Iris foetidissima *echo the strange sculptural shapes of the chestnut roots.*

Above: *Isabel Bannerman's sketch for one of the rustic temples within the Stumpery.*

Left: *The path under the archway is set with English ammonites and cobbles.*

Right: *One of a pair of green oak temples seen through the chestnut archway.*

Below Right: *'Goddess of the Woods' by the sculptor David Wynne sits in meditative pose in the grass clearing enclosed by the Stumpery.*

remotely finished. The visitors last week simply loved it – we
had to fight them off!'

There was much discussion about the inscriptions to
be carved on the wooden tablets at the back of the temples.
The Prince thought that one should be in Latin. Julian
Bannerman suggested that the Duke of Edinburgh's
unforgettable quote about the bonfire be translated, *Quando
haec ligna incenderentur?* but in the end more contemplative
texts were chosen: Shakespeare's 'Find tongues in trees, books
in running brooks, sermons in stone and good in everything,'
and Horace's 'They think that virtue is just a word and a
sacred grove merely sticks'.

The Prince originally commissioned the Stumpery as a refuge
for a serious collection of the hostas which he loves. His original
vision has expanded and now there are also collections of
hellebores, ferns and euphorbia growing there. On the Meadow
side there are blue hostas such as *H. sieboldiana* var. *elegans*,
'Halcyon', 'Hadspen Hawk', and *Euphorbia characias wulfenii*
and *E.* x *martinii.* There are also the Japanese painted ferns and
hellebore hybrids of the darkest slatey blue-black and green.
The root arch, where hart's-tongue, asplenium and dryopteris
ferns grow through the roots, leads into the glade. Here
hellebore hybrids of the clearest colours – yellow, claret, green,

Above: *The entablatures on the back of each temple display the use of wood as stone. On one, pine cones have been used as acroteria on top of the pediments and on the other, driftwood is made to look like flames.*

chocolate and rose – are mixed with spotted varieties and placed high upon the bank so that one can look up into the hearts of their pendant flowers. As the year progresses, hardy ferns unfurl in late spring along with the vivid green leaves of hostas such as 'Sum and Substance', 'Devon Green', 'Honeybells' and 'Royal Standard'. A dark background of butcher's broom (*Ruscus aculeatus*) planted along the top of the banks works to highlight the foreground, creating an especially rich contrast with the massed clumps of crown imperial fritillaries in spring and taller shrubs such as *Viburnum carlesii*. A wide selection of different varieties of mock orange has been planted to provide both flowers and scent throughout June in the stillness of the glade. Martagon lilies, already a feature of the woodland, flower above the architectural leaves of hostas in their prime. Beneath the oak tree in late summer cyclamens and autumn crocuses will emerge.

Right: *Green oak was used to construct the pair of temples which face east and west within the grove to gather the best of early morning and late evening sun.*

Beyond the Stumpery the Prince set stones around a shallow dip in the ground with a view to creating a moss garden. Eventually, a Japanese Garden was created there instead. The Prince was Patron of the Japan Festival and, as a gesture of gratitude, three gardeners were sent to Highgrove from Kyoto. A stone lantern shipped from Kyoto has been half-buried in the ground so that only its top is visible.

Part of the National Collection of Beeches has been planted between the Woodland Garden and the Wild Flower Meadow. The National Council for the Conservation of Plants and Gardens conserves the diversity of our plant heritage through its national collections. Highgrove now has more than seventy varieties of beech growing in the park. Near to the beeches, clumps of yellow and red dogwood backed by purple and orange willow have recently been planted. Their vivid stems provide the Prince with a colourful view from his bedroom window throughout the winter.

The Prince has always said that he needs a garden to delight the eye, warm the heart and feed the soul. 'I wanted my

Above: *In summer the Prince's growing collection of hostas takes over from the hellebores and euphorbias and fills the glade with a honeyed scent.*

Right: *Inside each temple are oak seats specially designed by the Bannermans after a hall seat by William Kent.*

Below Right: *A sketch by the Bannermans of the oak seat.*

garden to express in physical form what I feel at an inner level. I want it to be from the heart rather than the head.' When a group of Japanese businessmen from the Kowa Creative Art Company in Tokyo visited Highgrove in June 1996, they were given a tour of the garden and were very impressed by what they saw there. Their spokesman, Kozo Hoshino, wrote the following words in a letter written on behalf of the whole group to Mrs Simpson, their garden guide:

> Our client all enjoyed their visit to Highgrove and many thought it was highlight of our tour. Afterwards they kept talking about it. The Yamadas and I thought deeply of the garden and we agreed that Highgrove garden points out what 21 century concept of garden is all about. It represents this very form of culture in unmaterialistic embodiment called garden at its highest point and the most desirable form. Highgrove garden is certainly experience to open our eyes to what word garden really means. And important thing is that it express what Prince of Wales really is.

Left: *Driftwood, resembling vermiculated stone, fills the green oak pediment. Inside, the temples are lime rendered and washed with red ochres. There is an oak shingle roof behind the pediment.*

129

5 The Arboretum and Walled Garden

THE GREY-GREEN DOOR set in a Moorish arch of Cotswold stone can just be seen from the house across the Wild Flower Meadow. The door leads to the Walled Garden and was designed by the Prince, with inspiration from the Taj Mahal, to line up the view and end the vista. It is in fact a clever optical illusion, for as you get nearer you realize that the mown grass path leading you straight from the Sundial Garden ends several yards off centre. A small wooden gate painted in shades of buff and terracotta, colours chosen by the Prince from an eighteenth-century paint chart, heralds a path enclosed by a wavering serpentine hedge, which disguises the skew-whiff line to the Moorish arch. The hedge echoes the serpentine beech hedge at Chatsworth, one of the Prince's favourite places in the world and certainly a source of

Right: *Gates by William Bertram cross the main path to the Walled Garden from the house. The two inner posts can be lifted out to allow tractors to pass through.*

Right: *The view from the Azalea Walk towards the Wild Flower Meadow and the Sundial Garden. The spring planting in front of the serpentine hedge includes clumps of daffodils and tulips.*

Right: *The Arboretum, formerly a scruffy and overgrown plantation, which the Prince first began to tackle in 1992 under the direction of John White, who was then curator of neighbouring Westonbirt Arboretum.*

Below: Phlomis russeliana, *which abounds in summer, at the entrance to the Arboretum.*

Right: *Solid slate pots made by Joe Smith from Dumfries and given to the Prince who placed them at the entrance to the Arboretum.*

inspiration. The Highgrove hedge, however, is a tapestry of holly, privet, hawthorn, beech, cotoneaster and dogwood. Within its curvaceous shield are Christmas box, blocks of lush tulips in spring, and later in the year, towering Martagon lilies, hostas and high waves of yellow-flowered *Phlomis russeliana*. The phlomis came years ago from a friend at Shipton Moyne and has spread like Topsy.

Having walked across the Cotswold brash of the Meadow with its thin layer of topsoil, you suddenly find yourself on a narrow seam of the richest forest marble with a luscious topsoil 4ft deep. It runs on through Tetbury and out to the Home Farm, where David Wilson, the farm manager, is able to grow vegetables with ease in the fields that it crosses.

Above Left *and* **Right:** *The sweet gum tree,* Liquidambar styraciflua.

Opposite: *The leaves of Persian ironwood* Parrotia persica *glow in the foreground; beyond are the seven towering larches, part of the original planting before the Prince came.*

The eighteenth-century builders of Highgrove certainly knew where best to place the Walled Garden.

The Arboretum, with its great Autumn Walk swinging eastwards from the serpentine hedge, forms part of this island of deep soil. It is a bit like walking into Scotland. The towering larches 70ft high were planted in the 1950s. They may originally have been a screen against the road, but when the Prince decided to tackle this area in 1992 many had grown into scruffy specimens. He had always loved the neighbouring arboretum at Westonbirt, which has one of the finest collections of trees in the world. The Prince begged the advice of John White, then the curator of Westonbirt, to help him choose trees that would give outstanding autumn colour. John put forward various ideas in plan form. Among the hazels, ash and cherries are the rarer trees, exotic maples, such as *Acer palmatum*, which turns a purplish bronze in autumn, and the Katsura tree (*Cercidiphyllum japonicum*), which turns a butter yellow

Left: *Beech, hazel and an* Acer palmatum *in the foreground create a rich swathe of autumn colour in the Arboretum.*

Left: Acer palmatum 'Osakazuki'.

suffused with pink. After frost you can catch its burnt-sugar smell on the wind. There are also some variegated beeches such as *Fagus sylvatica* 'Aurea Marginata' and *F. s.* 'Silver Wood'.

Gradually, as the Prince's knowledge of trees grew, so did his desire to plant more and more unusual things, to replicate the technicolour autumn at Westonbirt. In June 1995 John White sketched out a planting plan for a new area: '...I am sure you will have some favourite plants you will want to use,' he wrote to the Prince, 'so I have not gone as far as a species list....We are looking for evergreens (8–10), medium flowering trees (about 5), small flowering trees (about 15).' On 9 July 1995 the Prince wrote a memo to John: 'Your suggestion looks splendid as I should very much like to try and plant some particularly interesting and rare trees if at all possible, and see if they could survive here! Kew gave me, for instance, a *Cladrastis lutea* the other day (good autumn colour they said!) and that might go in the new area? The most recent additions to the Arboretum are a manna ash (*Fraxinus ornus*) which bears a mass of white flowers, and some multi-stemmed eucalyptus.

At the end of the Autumn Walk is a sacred spot marked by the Sanctuary, which literally sprang from the ground over the last months of 1999. It was built to commemorate the Millennium and was blessed in January 2000 by the Bishop of London. From afar, when snow has just fallen, the sight of the tiny cruciform building immediately transports you to Russia. As you get nearer, however, it is clear that its materials are

Below: *The Sanctuary can just be seen beyond the larches, maples and box.*

reassuringly local. It instantly belongs and fits into this magical corner of a Gloucestershire glade. Built from earth blocks made from Highgrove clay and chopped barley straw, it is covered with a rich golden lime render, the base and dressings are all of local stone. The pitched oak roof has sweet chestnut sarking boards and is covered in Cotswold tiles. The basic principles for the Sanctuary were conceived by architect Keith Critchlow and founded on the sacred geometry of harmonic proportions, traditional in all ancient architecture and still used today in many eastern countries. Keith sent the Prince an explanatory piece from Plato's *Eponimus*:

Above: *The Sanctuary was built in 1999 to commemorate the Millennium as an expression of thanksgiving to God and was blessed in January 2000 by the Bishop of London.*

The way is this – for it is necessary to explain it thus far: every diagram, and system of number, and every combination of harmony, and the agreement of the revolution of the stars must be made manifest as one through all to him who learns in the proper way, and will be made manifest if, as we say, a man learns aright by keeping his gaze on unity: for it will be manifest to us, as we reflect, that there is one bond naturally uniting all these things: but if one goes about it in some other way, one must call on Fortune, as we also put it. For never without these lessons will any nature be happy in our cities…

Charles Morris worked up the design for the Sanctuary and it was built with unstinting attention to every detail by the same local firm from Berkeley who worked on the Orchard Room. 'Lighten our darkness we beseech thee O Lord' is inscribed in stone over the door. The eight capitols of the pale gold Farmington stone columns, four free-standing outside and four within, were carved by Dick Reid's studio at York. The design is simple and free flowing, depicting the leaves of the trees around the park and garden. Oaks, beeches, tulip trees, hollies, maples, birches, sweet chestnuts and willows are all included. The walls are pargetted with designs of vegetables from the garden as an expression of thanksgiving for all the good things God gives us. The stained-glass windows depict flowers and leaves from the garden and were painted by Shropshire artist John Napper and dedicated to the memory of Ted Hughes, the late poet laureate. Such love, care and thought by the Prince has gone into this building – it is a

fitting homage to God and the garden around it.

Towards the Spring Walk, spotted here and there with primroses, is a bronze sculpture of four girls in flowing dresses who seem to move among the trees. The *Daughters of Odessa* was made in remembrance of the innocent victims of repression in the twentieth century by American sculptor Frederick Hart. It was given to the Prince by the artist. The bluebell-edged ride continues back towards the Walled Garden, passing the hazels which the Prince and Prince Harry have recently coppiced. The coppicing will be repeated

Above: *The* Daughters of Odessa, *which stands at the end of the Spring Walk in the Arboretum, was sculpted by the American Frederick Hart and given by the artist to the Prince.*

Left: *The Azalea Walk in spring was created at the Prince's inspiration. The terracotta pots come from Ferone just outside Florence. It was the Prince's idea to thread various summer-flowering clematis through the azaleas.*

Above: *An Egyptian wall plaque set into the stone beside the Moorish arch.*

Right: *A statue of the goddess Diana commands the Azalea Walk. The yew hedge behind her has been shaped to echo the Moorish arch at the opposite end of the walk.*

Right: *Looking back from the secrecy of the Walled Garden through a faded pink door in the high wall and under a cascade of* Rosa *'Leverkusen', you glimpse the way through to the Arboretum beyond.*

throughout the Arboretum at seven-year intervals in the traditional way. The Prince is keen to revive the ancient tradition of coppicing woodland in Britain.

Ahead, over the ha-ha bridge, is a triumphal arch let into a cross-stepped dry-stone wall, displaying once again Fred Ind's and Paul Duckett's skills in carrying out the Bannerman's designs. Once through the arch you enter yet another country – instant Italy – magically conjured up by the Prince. It hardly feels like the Cotswolds. 'I have been inspired in different parts of the world,' he admits, 'and this walk of big pots with azaleas is taken from the Villa Gamberaia in Florence.' The pots come from Ferone just outside Florence and their scale is utterly right when combined with the high wall beside them which is scaled by the climbing roses 'Guinée', 'Penny Lane', 'Bobbie James' and 'Golden Showers', *Hydrangea petiolaris* and a Japanese wineberry. In spring, white and yellow scented azaleas such as *Rhododendron* 'Golden Oriole' and *R. exquisitum* grace the pots. It was the Prince's idea to thread clematis through them to give a summer display. The clematis varieties include, appropriately, 'Prince Charles' and 'Warszawska Nike'. At the southern end of the Azalea Walk a statue of the goddess Diana commands the scene with her bow and arrows. Behind her the yew hedge is cut in a perfect Moorish arch which mirrors the stone arch at the opposite end. It is the Prince who inspires these small architectural details that occur throughout the garden.

Through a faded pink door in the high wall and under a cascade of white roses, you enter the secrecy of the Walled Garden – perhaps the Prince's favourite place of all. It is a separate world. Within these high, mellow brick walls is

everything nostalgia ordered. You are suspended in time. The whole garden is on a gentle, south-facing slope. On a June evening there could hardly be anywhere more beautiful or more bountiful. The scale of everything feels inexplicably right and there is a rhythm about the flowing trees and flowers. Apple trees create cool tunnels that arch over hellebore-lined paths, sweet peas and runner beans smother arches of coppiced hazel and shade the little brick-edged, box-lined paths leading diagonally away; pink *Rosa mundi* spill over the box beside paths which lead towards arbours of white wisteria, roses, clematis and honeysuckle. Purple carrots, Red Salad Bowl lettuces, Charlotte potatoes and purple Brussels sprouts pack the patches to either side. Two of the vegetable patches are divided diagonally by a St Andrew's cross, the other two by the cross of St George.

A wide gravel path runs around the edge of the one-acre vegetable garden, beneath walls covered with roses, fan-trained nectarines, plums, cherries, apples and espalier pears. Tree lupins, aquilegia, billowings of senecio and all kinds of rosemaries spill out on to the pea gravel. A middle path leads to the centre of the garden, where water from the mossy fountain quietly gurgles and drips down two tiers into a round pool. Here water boatmen scud towards the reeds and mysterious koi carp, a present from Sir Yehudi Menuhin, loom beneath. A rosemary hedge encircles the space and sweet-smelling herbs like thyme, sage, rue and verbena spread through the gravel. Behind is a circle of 'Golden Hornet' crab apple trees, each one tied in to create a coronet. Abundant herbaceous borders stretch away north and south. Replanting during 2000 will include an incredible collection of salvias such as *Salvia confertiflora, S. leucantha, S. mexicana* and *S. involucrata.* A seat designed by Leon Krier is placed under the arbour smothered in the roses 'Etoile de Hollande' and 'Evangeline'. If you sit there for long enough, looking down the central herbaceous walk, you will see Marbled White butterflies, Tortoiseshells, Red Admirals, Meadow Browns and Holly Blues. The *genius loci* is here and

Left: *Senecio greyii billows out from under the wall below tumblings of the rose 'Bobbie James' softening the sharp-edged formality of the box–lined vegetable patches.*

Above: *The bronze wall plaque of the Green Man adorns a quiet corner in the Walled Garden. It was made by the sculptor Nicholas Dimbleby.*

147

the bronze plaque of the Green Man by Nicholas Dimbleby set
in a corner of the wall, commends him.

In 1980 this was a sorry patch. A large section of the north
wall had been knocked down to allow tractors to get in and
out when the garden was used for bulk potato production.
Many other sections of wall were missing as well. Nonetheless,
the Prince was captivated. As he wrote in *A Vision of Britain*:

Above: *Rampant sage
and rosemary beneath
espalier fruit trees spill
out on to the gravel path
along the western wall.*

148

One of the great pleasures of architecture is the feeling of well designed enclosure. It is an elementary idea with a thousand variants and can be appreciated at every level of building from the individual room to the interior of St Paul's Cathedral, or from the grand paved public square to the walled garden. The scale can be large or small, the material ancient or modern, but the cohesion, continuity and enclosure could produce a kind of magic. The application of these ideas makes the place unique....The secret of enclosed spaces is that they should have few entrances; if there are too many the sense of security disappears.

As a young boy spending long summers at Balmoral and Birkhall, the Prince loved to steal away to the secrecy of the kitchen garden whenever he had the chance. He had always wanted to grow his own vegetables. 'I loved the walled gardens then. I could potter about picking peas and eating them raw – and strawberries.' The Prince says that he knew nothing about gardening when he came to Highgrove, but in fact it was already in his blood. His grandmother is a legendary gardener and is President of the Garden Society. She and King George VI created her beautiful garden at Royal Lodge from scratch; her gardens at the Castle of Mey and Birkhall are exemplary and,

Below: Mysterious koi carp, a present from Sir Yehudi Menuhin, are half-hidden by water lilies in the pool.

Left: The moss-covered fountain in the centre of the Walled Garden is approached here through a cool tunnel of apples. Various herbs which surround the pool are allowed to spread informally.

Below: The Italian fountain after a frost.

though it may have been subconscious, the Prince undoubtedly absorbed their glory. As a young man, his first conscious inspiration was a walled garden at Crichel in Dorset which Lady Salisbury had helped to design.

Here at Highgrove the only answer was to bring a JCB into the Walled Garden and level the mess. It was a scratch job. The Prince and Lady Salisbury set about making plans on paper and deliberating for hours both at Cranborne and at Highgrove. The Prince's particular inspiration was the world-famous French garden at Villandry in the Loire Valley which was created in the late nineteenth century and is probably the

Right: *The vegetable patches are divided by brick paths lined with neatly clipped box and some are arched over with sweet peas and runner beans in summer.*

Above: Ornithogalum arabicum *blossom.*

Left: *Espaliered apples on iron supports form the main walk from east to west across the garden. They are underplanted with hellebores.*

Below Left: *The Prince picks from an apple tree.*

most complicated vegetable garden known to man. It was designed to employ hundreds of gardeners and to look glamorous and utterly contrived at all times. Vegetables were used entirely for pattern making and architecture. As a result, if you were to cut a cabbage from the wrong patch you would lose a vital bit of symmetry. The first plans for the vegetable garden at Highgrove were so complex that the Prince thought he would have to employ a one-legged gardener to hop from one small compartment to the next. The final design was a much simpler, more pleasing and more English version of Villandry. It is an extremely original and exceptionally beautiful way of combining artistry with the satisfactory production of fine fruit and vegetables.

The all-important structure of the garden took nearly two and a half years to complete. Its brick paths and the brick edges for the gravel paths were laid by Fred Ind and Cecil Gardiner. Cartloads of well-rotted manure were dumped in all the plots. By this time the Standing Garden, where plants are put temporarily, was full to the brim with things waiting to go in – many of them wedding presents for the Prince and Princess. Several of the fruit trees, for example, were a gift from the Worshipful Company of Fruiterers and the herbs were from the Sussex branch of the Women's Institute.

Of course, from the very beginning the garden has been managed organically. No plain sailing, particularly as far as the apples are concerned. Some of them are prone to canker and others to all kinds of rot. The Prince's attitude is to 'take the rough with the smooth', but the miracle worker behind the scenes is Dennis Brown. His vegetable growing is legendary across many counties. Taught by his father in the old school of gardening, he has never used chemicals, and buys nothing in save new types of vegetable seed. In 1984 Dennis, who lived close by at Badminton, was recommended by Paddy Whiteland as a genius of a vegetable grower. The Prince suggested that he came to work at Highgrove. 'He was a brave man to take me on,' admits Dennis Brown, who used to work for the Beaufort Hunt and the Atherstone before that. 'I'd worked with hounds for most of my life and I did gardening as a hobby. Mind you I

had won a lot of prizes at the big shows for my leeks and onions and so on.'

Dennis Brown wheels nearly a hundred wheelbarrow-loads of muck into the Walled Garden every year and in spring he digs it in. He is a natural and instinctive gardener. He does not follow rules or books. He is diligent, frugal and has an eye for beauty in the true cottage garden tradition. He uses soot to combat the slugs and likes to grow the vegetables and fruit that the Prince loves to eat rather than experimenting with rarities for the sake of it. 'He does love his Charlotte potatoes,'

Above: *Dennis Brown, the master vegetable grower, is in charge of the regiments of perfect vegetables.*

Right: *'Happil' strawberries, the Prince's favourite. The original plants were brought from Sandringham.*

says Dennis. He keeps a record of the sixteen plots within the Walled Garden, some of which crop twice a year, and thus he can carry out the right kind of rotation. For instance, he will plant spinach after spring cabbage and follow on with carrots. After early peas he plants leeks and after potatoes, lettuce. 'He is a miracle,' admits the Prince.

The door in the south wall is topped with obelisks. It leads past the rhubarb pots and the soft fruit cage, where the 'Happil' strawberries stop the greedy in their tracks.

The Rose Walk was inspired by a pergola seen in Iris Origo's garden which the Prince once visited in Tuscany. The Walk is spanned by the roses 'Pink Perpétué', 'Dublin Bay', 'Breath of Life', 'Paul's Himalayan Musk' and 'White Cockade'. The roses are intermingled with jasmine and the honeysuckles *Lonicera* x *americana*, the Late Dutch honeysuckle (*L. periclymenum* 'Serotina') and *L. periclymenum* 'Belgica'.

The Rose Walk leads back to the Azalea Walk to the east and west past the Standing Garden and towards the glasshouses. The first lean-to glasshouse is south facing. It is full to the brim with tree ferns, cyclamen, hoya, oranges, lemons and grapefruit trees, shocking pink Christmas cactus, jasmine, regal pelargoniums, orchids, clivias, daturas, 'Paper White' narcissi and hyacinths, all of them ready to fill the house when the Prince is at home. Under the staging, Dennis dries soil on plastic sacks. Later, the soil will become one of the ingredients in his own-recipe potting compost. Hanging from hooks are seed pods from which the seed will be gathered when it is

Above: *The Prince in the old greenhouse where plants for the house are brought on.*

Right: *A corner between the potting shed and the apple store where hazel sticks are stored, coppiced from the Arboretum and Highgrove woods.*

Right: *Geraniums are taken into the old greenhouse for overwintering. Still flowering in late autumn, they can be seen through the condensation on the glass.*

Above: *The new greenhouse which accommodates plants for the Orchard Room.*

Below: *The Rose Walk behind the Walled Garden was inspired by the Prince's visit to Iris Origo's garden in Tuscany.*

ripe. His show leeks are already planted in seed trays by November.

The new, north-facing Gothic greenhouse, painted whisper grey, was built in 1999 to accommodate plants needed to decorate the Orchard Room. Displayed on elegant wooden staging are stocks of caladium, leopard lilies, Swiss cheese plants, aspleniums, phalaenopsis, oncidium and cymbidium orchids and begonias grown for their foliage. The greenhouses are the domain of Gilly Hayward, a Somerset girl who tends and propagates all the new and replacement stock for the garden. She is so passionate about her rarer propagation successes that she treats them like children and asks after them fondly, long after they have gone out into the world. From the Courson Plant Fair near Paris she brought back a deep blue *Salvia discolor* which has a white fur on its leaves. From a single specimen she has produced forty plants.

Right: *Neat rows of 'Peer Gynt' Brussels sprouts in one of the box-lined beds of the Walled Garden.*

Below: *Dennis Brown achieves maximum effect by planting out the lettuce seedlings in rows of contrasting colours. Here 'Four Seasons', 'Lollo Rosso', 'Green Salad Bowl' and 'Red Salad Bowl' are almost ready for cutting.*

Above: *The grey-green leaves of 'Stuttgarter' onions are set off by a background of Senecio greyii.*

Above and **Right:**
A mixture of different apple varieties in store for the winter. Many of the apples from Highgrove are sent to the Priory, a local retirement home, and Tetbury hospital.

Left: *A selection of fruit and vegetables packed into a wheelbarrow bound for the kitchen at Highgrove.*

Overleaf: *The Walled Garden seen from above, showing the pattern of St George's crosses mixed with St Andrew's crosses. The Standing Garden lies beyond the south wall.*

Organic gardening is doubly difficult in a greenhouse. One slug can do horrendous damage and cups of beer don't always attract them away from the pelargoniums. In order to combat whitefly, Gilly gets parasitic wasps (*Encarssia formosa*) from the British Crop Protection Organization at Ashford in Kent. She feeds her plants with liquid comfrey, which she makes up herself, as well as blood, fish and bone meal.

At the back of the new greenhouse is the perfect potting shed. Its high windows face south, looking on to a little walled patch of ground where Dennis grows courgettes and Swiss chard and Gilly cultivates a thick row of comfrey along the west wall. Inside, there is a cool tin work surface under the window and every sign of industry. Plants are brought in to be split or potted on. In the gloom at the back of the shed are big bays of grit, sand and earth which Dennis riddles and then mixes with leaf mould for his compost.

Next to the potting shed, tucked into the corner of this little walled garden, is the tiny, two-storeyed apple store, perhaps the most exciting place in the whole garden. It consists of a cool, dark, cobble-floored room with a ladder which leads to the first floor. Here the apples are stored on large racks around the room. 'Formosa Nonpareil', 'Golden Knot', 'Cornish Aromatic' and 'Lady's Delight' are harvested from the trees beside the Orchard Room along with others gathered from the Walled Garden. Their smell is penetratingly nostalgic. 'A favourite place for the Princes when they were small,' remembers Dennis.

'…Perhaps the most amazing part of the garden in the time it has so quickly established, is the walled kitchen garden', wrote Victoria Verrier, the Taunton Parks and Amenities Officer, after her visit to Highgrove in June 1994. 'The box hedges, the apple arbours, the complete design I understand, all transpired from the Prince's eye for conservation, design and everything good about an Englishman's country garden.' And everything *is* good. In the end the love that the Prince puts into the garden is part of an act of the worship of God. He has created a microcosm to reflect the fundamental principles of the universe. Thirty years ago, when E. F. Schumacher caused such a stir with his book *Small is Beautiful*, people asked him 'What can I actually do?' He concluded: 'The answer is as simple as it is disconcerting: we can, each of us, work to put our own inner house in order. The guidance we need for this work cannot be found in science or technology, the value of which utterly depends on the ends they serve; but it can still be found in the traditional wisdom of mankind.'

Organic Gardening at Highgrove

by David Howard, Head Gardener

Our aim at Highgrove is to garden in harmony with Nature and not to contradict her laws. Over the past twenty years, several thousands of people have visited the farm and the garden and seen for themselves that it is possible to cultivate plants using methods that are in complete harmony with Nature, without resort to chemicals of any kind. The Prince's impressive achievement at Highgrove has earned him a reputation as a modern pioneer of the organic approach.

Few people understand the vital importance of soil to human life. At Highgrove, maintaining the fertility of the soil is our priority and we operate as closed a system as possible. Since my appointment, I have developed a system of compost making which creates a highly nutritious product in only twelve weeks, a useful turnaround.

My first task was to define our needs in the garden. Like anyone else, I had to decide what end product we wanted. A good, nutritious compost is required as a mulch for all of the flowerbeds. The mulch is spread on the surface of the soil so that the worms can gradually work it in. Unlike the majority of gardeners, our aim is always to feed the soil rather than the plant.

We try to be as self-sufficient as we can in the garden, buying in as little as possible. We have begun to make our own sowing and potting mixes and the compost produced in the garden has to be suitable for this purpose. The compost that goes into the potting mixes is exactly the same as that used as a mulch, except that it is sieved. In the future we may invest in a power screen. This is a sheet of 1-2in weld mesh. The compost is thrown through the mesh at high speed, which breaks it up very effectively.

The Highgrove composting system is unusual in that we distinguish between the different processes of decomposition in order to make different end products that are tailored to our specific needs. We use aerobic bacteria, which use the oxygen in the air to make the compost that is needed for mulches and potting mixes. In a separate bay we make leaf mould by harnessing anaerobic, fungal activity. The two products differ in nutrient content and structure and are put to entirely different uses in the garden.

There are very few other bodies investigating the production of pure leaf mould on such a large scale. We have discovered that we can produce a high-quality leaf mould in only a year, instead of the usual three year period. Traditionally, leaf mould is produced by anaerobic fungal activity alone. By adding a proportion of grass clippings and turning the heap regularly we have been able to combine fungal breakdown with a bacterial rotting action. The leaves are collected in a vacuum mower which partially chops them up. This also accelerates the rotting process as a greater surface area is exposed to fungus and bacteria.

Our leaf mould is completely different from the compost that we produce in the neighbouring bay. It is very low in nutrients, but very fibrous. We use it like peat, which it resembles in many ways. Like the compost, leaf mould forms an essential part of our own potting mixes.

Shortly after I was appointed we purchased a mechanical digger. It is a very small machine which can be driven into the compost bays and used to turn the compost once a week. This way we incorporate more air, accelerating the rotting process. We also incorporate straw into the heap as this balances the ratio of carbon to nitrogen and prevents grass clippings from turning into a sticky sludge. By this method we are able to produce high-quality compost in as little as twelve weeks.

Despite the temperature inside the heap, which can be as high as 80°C in summer, we do not compost pernicious perennial weeds. Experience has taught me that bindweed, ground elder, thistles and docks are well able to survive the composting process.

During the winter the heap can be slow to heat up. When this happens we use poultry manure as an accelerator. We also insulate the heap by pushing straw between the slats of the bins as well as covering its top.

Our home-produced potting and seed mixes are proving very successful. Commercial composts contain chemicals that promote rapid growth. Seedlings raised in a commercial compost grow rapidly and are often very sappy. This makes them particularly vulnerable when they are planted out. We aim to produce a slow-release, nitrogen-rich growing medium. If extra nitrogen is required we use organic substances such as fish, blood and bone. On the whole, it is only plants that are going to spend two or three years in a pot that require additional feeding. The garden plants thrive on the compost mulch that is gradually incorporated into the soil by earthworms. Greenhouse and pot plants are also given liquid feeds which we produce ourselves.

Many people fear that by adopting the organic approach they will be left without weapons in the battle against garden pests and diseases. When we remove synthetic weapons, such as herbicides, fungicides and insecticides, from the garden we have to make much more use of our own initiative. At Highgrove we observe all of our plants very carefully and note their natural level of resistance to disease. Among the roses, for example, we have found that *Rosa mundi* is very resistant, as are most of the *Rosa rugosa* family. The Gallica rose 'Tuscany Superb' drops its leaves at the first sign of blackspot, while 'Charles de Mills', also a Gallica, is far more resistant. We apply the same process to our choice of fruit trees. Perhaps the most important thing of all is our belief that perfection is only something to be aimed at and rarely achieved.

After twenty years of organic gardening there is a natural harmony that works to keep pests down to tolerable levels. Slugs pose little problem as the birds keep them in check. In the glasshouses we use hand-picking and introduced predators to keep pests under control. Like the sharp sand in our potting mixes, these predatory insects have to be bought in. They have proved to be very much cheaper than chemical treatments. Along with the bulbs bought in each spring, the predatory insects and the sand are some of the very few things that we bring into the garden.

When I show groups around the garden, people often ask me how they can apply our methods in their own gardens. I always explain that it just a matter of scaling things down a bit and ensuring that their own plot is managed in an enviro-friendly, organic way. Whatever you choose to call it, it all comes down to the same thing. It means working with the forces of Nature and always abiding by her laws. The most important thing is the soil. If everyone looked after their own little patch there would be no problem.

Organic gardening is not difficult, but you must always bear in mind that you are only ever aiming for perfection. Your aim should be to create a garden that is in harmony. If you have a problem in the garden, look to Nature for the answer. I have tremendous faith in Nature, and this is what gives me the confidence to run the garden at Highgrove for the Prince.

Further information on organic gardening can be readily obtained from the Henry Doubleday Research Association at Wolston Lane, Ryton on Dunsmore, Coventry CV8 3LG.

Plant Listings

This list is complementary to those plants mentioned in the book, but it is not comprehensive.

The View from the House

Sundial Garden

BEDS

Buxus sempervirens

Tulipa 'Black Parrot' Bulb

Viola cornuta 'Alba' Perennial

Convallaria majalis Perennial

Helleborus orientalis (white form)
  Evergreen perennial

Convolvulus cneorum Evergreen
  shrub

Aquilegia 'Magpie' Perennial

Tulipa 'Queen of Night' Bulb

T. 'Maureen' Bulb

Verbascum phoeniceum 'Album'
  Perennial

Phlox paniculata alba Perennial

Ophiopogon planiscapus 'Nigrescens'
  Evergreen perennial

Agapanthus africanus 'Albus' Perennial

Lunaria annua 'Alba Variegata' Annual

Heuchera 'Plum Puddin' Evergreen
  perennial

H. 'Chocolate Ruffles' Evergreen
  perennial

Clematis recta Perennial

Geranium phaeum 'Album' Perennial

Lupinus 'Polar Princess' Perennial

Gypsophila Perennial

Pittosporum tenuifolium 'Tom Thumb'
  Evergreen shrub

Parahebe Evergreen shrub

Primula denticulata Perennial

Aquilegia 'William Guinness' Perennial

Helleborus torquatus Perennial

Iris chrysographes Rhizome

Digitalis purpurea albiflora Biennial

Spiraea nipponica 'Snowmound'
  Deciduous shrub

Viola 'Molly Sanderson' Perennial

V. 'Springtime Black' Perennial

Rosa Iceberg Deciduous shrub

Eupatorium rugosum 'Chocolate'
  Perennial

Geranium clarkei 'Kashmir White'
  Perennial

Papaver orientale 'Perry's White'
  Perennial

Scabiosa 'Ace of Spades' Perennial

Salvia discolor Semi-evergreen
  perennial

Aster latiflorus 'Lady in Black'
  Perennial

Aquilegia vulgaris 'Munstead White'
  Perennial

Dianthus 'Mrs Sinkins' Perennial

Exochorda x *macrantha* 'The Bride'
  Deciduous shrub

Aquilegia 'Black Barlow' Perennial

Lysimachia clethroides Perennial

Pulsatilla vulgaris 'Alba' Perennial

Lablab 'Black Knight' Annual

Tulipa 'White Dream' Bulb

Galanthus 'S. Arnott' Bulb

Anthriscus sylvestris 'Ravenswing'
  Perennial

Hydrangea arborescens 'Annabelle'
  Deciduous shrub

Berberis thunbergii 'Helmond Pillar'
  Evergreen shrub

Lamium maculatum 'White Nancy'
  Perennial

Iris 'Black Swan' Bulb

Alcea rosea 'Nigra' Perennial

Polemonium caeruleum var. *album*
  Perennial

Malva moschata f. *alba* Perennial

Tulipa 'Mount Tacoma' Bulb

Cornus alba 'Kesselringii' Deciduous
  shrub

Dahlia 'Bishop of Llandaff' Bulb

Clematis florida 'Seiboldii' Deciduous
  climber

Clematis 'Early Sensation' Deciduous
  climber

Sundial Garden

HOUSE BORDER

Viburnum x *bodnantense* Deciduous
  shrub

Fremontodendron Semi-evergreen shrub

Physocarpus opulifolius 'Diabolo'
  Deciduous shrub

Iris unguicularis Bulb

Jasminum officinale Deciduous climber

Choisya 'Aztec Pearl' Evergreen shrub

Solanum crispum 'Glasnevin' Deciduous
  climber

Sambucus 'Black Knight' Deciduous
  shrub

Rosa 'Madame Hardy' Deciduous shrub

Viburnum tinus Evergreen shrub

Euonymus fortunei 'Emerald Gaiety'

House front

Rosa 'Mermaid' Deciduous climber

Jasminum nudiflorum Deciduous shrub

Vitis coignetiae Deciduous climber

Hedera colchica 'Paddy's Pride' Evergreen
  climber

Mahonia japonica Evergreen shrub

Rosa 'Felicia' Deciduous shrub

Senecio 'Sunshine' Evergreen shrub

Viburnum davidii Evergreen shrub

Quercus ilex Evergreen tree

Terrace

Prunus lusitanica Evergreen tree

Choisya ternata Evergreen shrub

Smilacina racemosa Perennial

Rosa 'Pearl Drift' Deciduous shrub

Senecio 'Sunshine' Evergreen shrub

Helleborus orientalis hybrids Evergreen
  perennial

Viburnum carlesii 'Aurora' Deciduous
  shrub

V. x *carlcephalum* Deciduous shrub

Euphorbia myrsinites Evergreen
  perennial

Anaphalis triplinervis Perennial

Olearia x *scilloniensis* Evergreen shrub

Hebe ochracea 'James Stirling' Evergreen shrub

Rosa 'Sander's White Rambler' (weeping standard) Deciduous shrub

Echinops ritro Perennial

Philadelphus coronarius 'Aureus' Deciduous shrub

Lonicera pericyclamen 'Graham Thomas' Deciduous climber

Aucuba japonica 'Crotonifolia' Evergreen shrub

Alchemilla mollis Perennial

Melissa officinalis 'All Gold' Perennial

Acid Bed

Arisaema candidissimum Perennial

Erythronium 'Pagoda' Perennial

Gentiana speciosum Perennial

Lilium regale Perennial

Corydalis solida Perennial

Galium odoratum Perennial

Wisteria floribunda Deciduous climber

Rosa 'Wedding Day' Deciduous climber

Mitraria coccinea 'Lake Puje' Evergreen climber

Fountain Garden

CLOCKWISE FROM GLADIATOR

Origanum vulgare 'Aureum' Perennial

Verbena bonariensis Perennial

Achillea filipendulina 'Gold Plate Perennial

Salvia officinalis 'Icterina' Perennial

S. candelabrum Evergreen shrub

Perovskia atriplicifolia Perennial

Rosa 'Charles de Mills' (Gallica) Deciduous shrub

R. 'Cardinal de Richlieu' (Gallica) Deciduous shrub

Lavandula stoechas Evergreen shrub

Teucrium fruticans Perennial

Nepeta x *faassenii* Perennial

Rosa 'Tuscany Superb' (Gallica) Deciduous shrub

R. Winchester Cathedral Deciduous shrub

R. 'Charles de Mills' (Gallica) Deciduous shrub

Iris barbata 'Leda's Lover' Perennial

The Cottage Garden

Pergola

Clematis 'Mrs George Jackman' Deciduous climber

Rosa 'Crimson Glory' Deciduous shrub

Clematis campaniflora Deciduous climber

C. 'Comtesse de Bouchard' Deciduous climber

Rosa 'Blairi Number Two' Deciduous shrub

R. 'Zéphirine Drouhin' Deciduous shrub

Clematis chinensis Deciduous climber

Rosa 'Gloire de Dijon' Deciduous shrub

R. 'Guinée' Deciduous shrub

R. 'Etoile de Hollande' Deciduous shrub

Clematis viticella 'Polish Spirit' Deciduous climber

C. 'Madame Julia Correvon' Deciduous climber

Rosa 'Cécile Brunner' Deciduous shrub

Clematis 'Madame Julia Correvon' Deciduous climber

C. 'Ascotiensis' Deciduous climber

Box Garden

Buxus 'Argenteovariegata' Evergreen tree

B. 'Blauer Heinz' Evergreen tree

B. 'Faulkner' Evergreen tree

B. 'Greenpeace' Evergreen tree

B. 'Green Velvet' Evergreen tree

B. 'Latifolia Maculata' Evergreen tree

B. 'Memorial' Evergreen tree

B. 'Morris Midget' Evergreen tree

B. 'Rotundifolia' Evergreen tree

B. 'Suffruticosa' Evergreen tree

Swimming Pool Gate – Cottage Garden Entrance

Sarcococca confusa Evergreen shrub

Morus nigra Deciduous tree

Helleborus 'Dick Grandon' Evergreen perennial

H. 'Phylly' Evergreen perennial

H. 'Joan Bridges' Evergreen perennial

Brunnera macrophylla 'Variegata' Perennial

Epimedium davidii Evergreen perennial

Rhamnus alaternus 'Argenteovariegata' Evergreen shrub

Phlomis russeliana Evergreen perennial

Veratrum nigrum Perennial

Acanthus mollis Perennial

Bergenia sp. Evergreen perennial

Kniphofia sp. Perennial

Pyrus salicifolia 'Pendula' Deciduous tree

Rubus thibetanus Deciduous shrub

Viburnum tinus Deciduous shrub

Salvia involucrata 'Bethellii' Perennial

Limonium latifolium Perennial

Sisyrinchium striatum Evergreen perennial

Helleborus subsp. *guttatus* Evergreen perennial

Magnolia x *loebneri* 'Leonard Messel' Deciduous shrub

Island Bed

Acer pensylvanicum Deciduous tree

Sedum spectabile 'Autumn Joy' Perennial

Clematis 'Niobe' Perennial

Cephalaria alpina Perennial

Phlomis russeliana Evergreen perennial

Helleborus x *sternii* Evergreen perennial

Viburnum x *globosum* 'Jermyns Globe' Evergreen shrub

Liriodendron tulipifera 'Aureomarginatum' Deciduous tree

Stachys lanata 'Silver Carpet' Ground cover

Ligustrum japonicum 'Rotundifolium' Evergreen shrub

Hebe ochracea 'James Stirling' Evergreen shrub

Taxus baccata 'Fastigiata' Evergreen tree

Rosa 'Souvenir de St. Anne's' Deciduous shrub

Penstemon 'Evelyn' Perennial

Phormium tenax   Evergreen perennial
Rosa 'Gertrude Jekyll'   Deciduous shrub
Lysimachia clethroides   Perennial
Iris chrysographes   Perennial
Catanache caerulea   Perennial
Sisyrinchium striatum   Perennial
Allium hollandicum 'Purple Sensation'
    Bulb
Clematis heracleifolia 'Wyevale'   Perennial
Anaphalis triplinervis   Perennial
Rosa 'Ballerina'   Deciduous shrub
Lobelia laxiflora var. *angustifolia*
    Perennial
Viburnum carlesii 'Diana'   Deciduous
    shrub
Euphorbia griffithii 'Fireglow'   Perennial
Angelica archangelica   Perennial
Smyrnium perfoliatum   Biennial
Choisya ternata 'Sundance'   Evergreen
    shrub

Barn Wall Bed

Acer griseum   Deciduous tree
Helleborus foetidus   Deciduous shrub
Abeliophyllum distichum   Evergreen
    perennial
Schisandra sphenanthera   Deciduous
    climber
Viburnum rhytidophyllum   Evergreen
    shrub
Arbutus unedo   Evergreen shrub
Lunaria annua 'Purpurea'   Annual
Aralia elata 'Albomarginata'   Deciduous
    tree
Knautia macedonica   Perennial
Thermopsis caroliniana   Perennial
Bupleurum fruticosum   Evergreen shrub
Chimonanthus praecox   Deciduous shrub
Nandina domestica   Semi-evergreen
    shrub
Ribes speciosum   Semi-evergreen shrub
Piptanthus nepalensis   Deciduous shrub
Soleirolia soleirolii   Ground cover
Leycesteria formosa   Deciduous shrub
Phygelius x *rectus* 'Winchester Fanfare'
    Semi-evergreen shrub
Melianthus major   Perennial

Angelica archangelica   Perennial
Prunus 'Taihaku'   Deciduous tree
Viburnum x *globosum* 'Jermyns Globe'
    Evergreen shrub
Osmanthus delavayi   Evergreen shrub
Azara microphylla   Evergreen shrub
Paeonia sp. (tree peony)   Deciduous
    shrub
Trochodendron aralioides   Evergreen
    shrub
Hydrangea petiolaris   Deciduous climber
Clematis 'Madame Edouard André'
    Deciduous climber
Rosa 'The Pilgrim'   Deciduous shrub
Hydrangea quercifolia 'Snow Queen'
    Deciduous shrub
Euphorbia characias   Evergreen
    perennial
Lonicera lanceolata   Evergreen climber
Dicentra spectabilis 'Alba'   Perennial
Morus nigra   Deciduous tree

Rose Arch – Pergola Left Side

Viburnum tinus 'Eve Price'   Evergreen
    shrub
Taxus baccata 'Fastigiata'   Evergreen tree
Viburnum x *juddii*   Evergreen shrub
Ornithogalum arabicum   Bulb
Nepeta x *faassenii*   Perennial
Rosa 'Little White Pet' (standard)
    Deciduous shrub
Narcissus 'Cheerfulness'   Bulb
Delphinium sp.   Perennial
Tulipa 'Spring Green'   Bulb
Narcissus 'Trevithian'   Bulb
Humulus lupulus 'Aureus'   Deciduous
    climber
Campanula lactiflora   Perennial
Tradescantia virginiana   Perennial
Lobelia x *gerardii* 'Vedrariensis'
    Perennial
Hosta (hybrids in variety)   Perennial
Actinidia deliciosa 'Hayward'   Deciduous
    climber
Philadelphus   Deciduous shrub
Alchemilla mollis   Perennial
Narcissus 'Telamonius Plenus'   Bulb

Fritillaria imperialis   Bulb
Narcissus 'Mount Hood'   Bulb
N. 'Cheerfulness'   Bulb
Tulipa 'White Dream'   Bulb
T. 'Mount Tacoma'   Bulb
Monarda 'Ou Charm'   Perennial
Origanum laevigatum   Perennial
Cistus 'Peggy Sammons'   Evergreen shrub

Rose Arch – Pergola Right Side

Hydrangea arborescens 'Annabelle'
    Deciduous shrub
Nepeta x *faassenii*   Perennial
Rosa 'Little White Pet' (standard)
    Deciduous shrub
Leucanthemum x *superbum*   Perennial
Juniperus communis 'Hibernica'
    Perennial
Hebe 'Red Edge'   Evergreen shrub
Foeniculum vulgare 'Purpureum'
    Perennial
Rosa 'Iceberg'   Deciduous shrub
Knautia macedonica   Perennial
Aster novi-belgii 'Orlando'   Perennial
Monarda 'Ou Charm'   Perennial
Rosa glauca   Deciduous shrub
Acanthus mollis   Perennial
Spiraea 'Arguta'   Deciduous shrub
Phlomis russeliana   Semi-evergreen
    perennial
Taxus baccata 'Fastigiata'   Evergreen tree
Campanula persicifolia   Perennial
Sorbus thibetica 'John Mitchell'
    Deciduous tree

Entrance to Cottage Garden – Holm Oak

Phlomis russeliana   Evergreen perennial
Morina longifolia   Perennial
Rosa glauca (syn. *R. rubrifolia*)
    Deciduous shrub
Hydrangea quercifolia   Deciduous shrub
Stipa gigantea   Deciduous grass
Penstemon 'Russian River'   Perennial
Kniphofia 'Yellow Hammer'   Perennial
Cephalaria gigantea   Perennial
Ligularia stenocephala   Perennial
Phormium tenax   Evergreen perennial

Viburnum x *hillieri* Evergreen shrub
Zantedeschia aetheopica Perennial
Pittosporum tenuifolium 'Silver Queen'
  Evergreen shrub
Agapanthus sp. Perennial
Choisya 'Aztec Pearl' Evergreen shrub
Hydrangea arborescens 'Annabelle'
  Deciduous shrub
Helleborus x *sternii* Evergreen perennial

**From Garden Entrance to Laurel
  Tunnel**
BULBS IN GRASS
Camassia leichtlinii Bulb
Narcissus 'Ice Follies' Bulb
N. 'Carlton' Bulb
N. 'Pheasant's Eye' Bulb
N. 'Trevithian' Bulb
Rosa 'Paul's Himalayan Musk' Deciduous
  climber
R. 'Rambling Rector' Deciduous climber
R. 'Seagull' Deciduous climber
Cornus mas Deciduous shrub
Berberis julianae Evergreen shrub
Elaeagnus x *ebbingei* Evergreen shrub
Magnolia var. *borealis* 'Lilenny'
  Deciduous tree
Ribes laurifolium Deciduous shrub
Viburnum davidii Evergreen shrub
Sorbus matsumurana Deciduous tree
Betula pendula 'Youngii' Deciduous tree
Lonicera fragrantissima Deciduous shrub
Catalpa bignonioides 'Aurea' Deciduous
  tree
Prunus 'Ukon' Deciduous tree
Garrya elliptica Evergreen shrub
Viburnum plicatum Deciduous shrub
Mahonia 'Winter Sun' Evergreen shrub
Cotoneaster x *wateri* 'Exburiensis'
  Deciduous shrub
Parrotia persica Deciduous tree
Leycesteria formosa Deciduous shrub
Pulmonaria rubra Perennial
Geranium sp. Perennial
Lonicera pileata Evergreen shrub
Rosa 'Canary Bird' Deciduous shrub
Lunaria annua 'Alba Variegata' Biennial

Lobelia cardinalis 'Queen Victoria'
  Perennial

Wild Flower Meadow and Woodland Garden

Tulip Walk
Carpinus betulus 'Fastigiata' Deciduous
  tree
Tulipa 'Queen of Night' Bulb
T. 'Attila' Bulb
T. 'Negrita' Bulb
Camassia leichtlinii Bulb
Ilex aquifolium 'Ferox Argentea'
  Evergreen shrub
Acer palmatum 'Fireglow' Deciduous tree
Prunus lusitanica 'Variegata' Evergreen shrub
Fritillaria meleagris Bulb

Southern Hemisphere Garden
Cordyline australis Evergreen tree
Phormium tenax 'Variegatum' Evergreen
  perennial
Pittosporum bicolor Evergreen shrub
Eucalyptus pauciflora Evergreen tree
Phormium tenax Evergreen perennial
Hydrangea villosa Deciduous shrub
Eucalyptus gunnii Evergreen tree
Paulownia tomentosa Deciduous tree
Trachycarpus fortuneii Evergreen shrub
Dicksonia antarctica Fern
D. fibrosa Fern
Blechnum chilense Fern
Phormium cookianum Evergreen
  perennial
P. tenax 'Nanum Purpureum' Evergreen
  perennial
Cyathea australis

Stumpery
Cyclamen hederifolium Bulb
Erythronium 'Pagoda' Bulb
Polypodium glycyrrhiza Fern
Fritillaria imperialis Bulb
Ruscus aculeatus Evergreen shrub
Helleborus argutifolius Evergreen
  perennial

Gymnocarpium dryopteris Evergreen
  perennial
Helleborus foetidus Evergreen perennial
Ribes laurifolium Evergreen shrub
Polypodium cambricum 'Richard Kayse'
  Fern
Helleborus orientalis 'Orion' Perennial
Dryopteris affinis 'Cristata' Fern
D. x *complexa ramosissima* 'Weight' Fern
Daphne laureola Evergreen shrub
Hosta 'Devon Green' Perennial
H. 'Golden Sunburst' Perennial
H. 'Invincible' Perennial
H. 'Green Acres' Perennial
H. 'Love Pat' Perennial

Woodland Garden
Lonicera pileata Evergreen shrub
Eleagnus Evergreen shrub
Heracleum mantegazzianum Perennial
Euonymus japonicus 'Macrophyllus Albus'
  Evergreen shrub
Viburnum plicatum Deciduous shrub
Lunaria annua Annual
Vinca major Evergreen perennial
Phildelphus 'Manteau d' Hermine'
  Deciduous shrub
P. 'Beauclerk' Deciduous shrub
Cornus stolonifera 'Flaviramea'
  Deciduous shrub
Hypericum Semi-evergreen shrub
Syringa vulgaris 'Madame Lemoine'
  Deciduous shrub
Hydrangea villosa Deciduous shrub
Ligustrum ovlifolium 'Aureum'
  Deciduous shrub
Pulmonaria rubra Groundcover
Hosta 'Frances Williams' Perennial
H. 'Krossa Regal' Perennial
H. 'Prince of Wales' Perennial
H. 'Sum and Substance' Perennial
H. undulata var. *undulata* Perennial
H. 'Sagae' Perennial
H. 'Green Acres' Perennial
H. 'Invincible' Perennial
H. 'Francee' Perennial
Choisya ternata Evergreen shrub

Forsythia x *intermedia* 'Lynwood' Deciduous shrub

Magnolia Deciduous shrub

Colutea persica Deciduous shrub

Dicentra spectabilis 'Alba' Perennial

The Arboretum and Walled Garden

Serpentine Hedge

Sarcococca confusa Evergreen shrub

S. hookeriana var. *humilis* Evergreen shrub

S. h. var. *digyna* Evergreen shrub

Lilium martagon Bulb

Hosta lancifolia Perennial

H. 'Halcyon' Perennial

Ligularia 'The Rocket'

Phygelius 'Winchester Fanfare' Semi-evergreen shrub

P. x *rectus* 'Moonraker' Semi-evergreen shrub

Pimpinella major 'Rosea' Perennial

Phlomis russeliana Evergreen perennial

Sisyrinchium striatum Evergreen perennial

Hemerocallis sp. Perennial

Kniphofia 'Green Jade' Perennial

Acorus gramineus 'Variegatus' Semi-evergreen waterplant.

Narcissus 'Jack Snipe' Bulb

Asplenium scolopendrium Semi-evergreen fern

Arboretum

Liquidambar styraciflua Deciduous tree

Viburnum plicatum 'Mariesii' Deciduous shrub

Euodia daniellii Deciduous tree

Parrotia persica Deciduous tree

Corylus avellana Deciduous tree

Acer palmatum 'Senkaki' Deciduous tree

A.p. 'Elegans' Deciduous tree

A.p. 'Bloodgood' Deciduous tree

A.p. 'Butterfly' Deciduous tree

A.p. 'Osakazuki' Deciduous tree

A.p. 'Ornatum' Deciduous tree

A.p. 'Atropurpureum' Deciduous tree

A.p. 'Hessei' Deciduous tree

Acer japonicum 'Vitifolium' Deciduous tree

A. j. 'Aconitifolium' Deciduous tree

A. shirasawanum 'Aureum' Deciduous tree

Abies veitchii Evergreen conifer

Euonymus alatus Deciduous shrub

Cercidiphyllum japonicum Deciduous tree

Betula utilis var. 'Jacquemontii' Deciduous tree

Tsuga heterophylla Evergreen conifer

Osmanthus delavayi Evergreen shrub

Cryptomeria japonica Evergreen conifer

Metasequoia glyptostroboides Deciduous conifer

Cornus 'Porlock' Deciduous shrub

Cercidiphyllum japonicum Deciduous tree

Laburnocytisus adamii Deciduous tree

Fraxinus ornus Deciduous tree

Liriodendron tulipifera Deciduous tree

Sequoiadendron giganteum Evergreen conifer

Calocedrus decurrens Evergreen conifer

Ginkgo biloba Deciduous conifer

Cornus mas Deciduous shrub

Osmanthus serrulatus Evergreen shrub

Ilex aquifolium 'Madame Briot' Evergreen shrub

Abies grandis Evergreen conifer

Cornus alba 'Elegantissima' Deciduous shrub

Juniperus virginiana Evergreen conifer

Pyrus cordata Deciduous tree

Acer henryi Deciduous tree

Magnolia dawsoniana Deciduous shrub

Sorbus commixta 'Embley' Deciduous tree

Abies nordmanniana Evergreen conifer

Picea omorika Evergreen conifer

Malus sylvestris Deciduous tree

Quercus suber Evergreen tree

Cercis siliquastrum Deciduous shrub

Acer macrophyllum Deciduous tree

Garrya elliptica 'James Roof' Evergreen shrub

Castanea sativa 'Argenteovariegata' Deciduous tree

Hamamelis x *intermedia* 'Pallida' Deciduous shrub

Hydrangea petiolaris Deciduous climber

Azalea Walk

Rhododendron basilicum Deciduous shrub

R. 'Golden Oriole' Deciduous shrub

R. 'Daviesii' Deciduous shrub

R. 'Exquisita' Deciduous shrub

R. 'Golden Dream' Deciduous shrub

R. delicatissimum Deciduous shrub

Clematis 'Prince Charles' (blue) Deciduous climber

C. 'Niobe' (red) Deciduous climber

ROSES

Rosa 'Gloire de Dijon' Deciduous climber

R. 'Kathleen Harrop' Deciduous climber

R. 'May Queen' Deciduous climber

R. 'Rosy Mantle' Deciduous climber

R. Penny Lane Deciduous climber

R. 'Perpetually Yours' Deciduous climber

R. 'Albéric Barbier' Deciduous climber

R. 'Parade' Deciduous climber

R. 'Golden Showers' Deciduous climber

R. 'Sympathie' Deciduous climber

WALL CLIMBERS

Humulus lupulus 'Aureus' Deciduous climber

Hedera colchica Evergreen climber

Vitis coignetiae Deciduous climber

Actinidia kolomikta Deciduous climber

Actinidia chinensis Deciduous climber

Clematis montana sp. Deciduous climber

C. hookeriana 'Huldine' Deciduous climber

Hydrangea petiolaris Deciduous shrub

Pyracantha Evergreen shrub

Jasminum nudiflorum Evergreen shrub

Walled Garden

WALL FRUIT AND ROSES

Rosa 'Leverkusen' Deciduous shrub

Apple – 'Cox's Orange Pippin' Deciduous tree

Damson – 'Merryweather' Deciduous tree

Pear – 'Beurré Hardy' Deciduous tree

Pear – 'Williams' bon Chrétien' Deciduous tree

Plum – 'Jefferson' Deciduous tree

Plum – 'Green Gage' Deciduous tree

Cherry – 'Morello' Deciduous tree

Cherry – 'Stella' Deciduous tree

Rosa 'Madame Alfred Carrière' Deciduous shrub

Gage – 'Willingham' Deciduous tree

Plum – 'Victoria' Deciduous tree

Plum – 'Herman' Deciduous tree

Rosa 'Emily Gray' Deciduous tree

Plum – 'Kirke's Blue' Deciduous tree

Nectarine – 'Lord Napier' Deciduous tree

Rosa 'Etoile de Hollande' Deciduous tree

Pear – 'Concorde' Deciduous tree

Pear – 'Conference' Deciduous tree

Plum – 'Marjorie's Seedling' Deciduous tree

Peach – 'Duke of York' Deciduous tree

Plum – 'Opal' Deciduous tree

Cherry – 'Florence' Deciduous tree

Peach – 'Peregrine' Deciduous tree

Pear – 'Winter Nelis' Deciduous tree

Apricot – 'Moor Park' Deciduous tree

Pear – 'Pitmaston Duchess' Deciduous tree

Pear – 'Doyenné de Comice' Deciduous tree

ESPALIER APPLES

'Spartan' Deciduous tree

'American Mother' Deciduous tree

'Edward VII' Deciduous tree

'Norfolk Royal Russet' Deciduous tree

'Jupiter' Deciduous tree

'Grenadier' Deciduous tree

'Sturmer Pippin' Deciduous tree

'Michaelmas Red' Deciduous tree

'Ribston Pippin' Deciduous tree

'Gloster 69' Deciduous tree

'Reverend W. Wilks' Deciduous tree

'Elstar' Deciduous tree

'Arthur Turner' Deciduous tree

'Golden Delicious' Deciduous tree

'Egremont Russet' Deciduous tree

Pear – 'Glou Morceau' Deciduous tree

DOMES

Clematis montana Deciduous climber

Wisteria sinensis Deciduous climber

Lonicera periclymenum 'Belgica' Deciduous climber

Rosa 'Francis E. Lester' Deciduous shrub

Rosa 'Paul's Himalayan Musk' Deciduous shrub

Rosa 'Adélaide d'Orléans' Deciduous shrub

WALL BEDS CLOCKWISE FROM AZALEA WALK ENTRANCE

Ruta graveolens Evergreen shrub

Lepechinia salviae Perennial

Spiraea 'Goldflame' Deciduous shrub

Salvia turkestanica Perennial

Santolina chamaecyparissus Evergreen shrub

Senecio 'Sunshine' Evergreen shrub

Salvia officinalis Evergreen shrub

S. o. 'Purpurascens' Evergreen shrub

S. o. 'Icterina' Evergreen shrub

Helleborus foetidus Evergreen perennial

Dianthus 'Doris' Evergreen perennial

Ballota acetabulosa Evergreen perennial

Artemesia 'Powis Castle' Evergreen shrub

Cistus pulverulentus 'Sunset' Evergreen shrub

C. x *purpureus* Evergreen shrub

Sisyrinchium striatum 'Aunt May' Evergreen perennial

Salvia candelabrum Semi-evergreen perennial

Chimonanthus praecox Deciduous shrub

Campanula glomerata 'Superba' Perennial

Sedum spectabile 'Autumn Joy' Perennial

Sisyrinchium montanum nudicaule Evergreen perennial

Myrtus communis Evergreen shrub

Fragaria Pink Panda Evergreen perennial

Geranium sanguineum 'Album' Perennial

Phlomis italica Evergreen shrub

P. longifolia Evergreen shrub

Salvia pratensis Perennial

CENTRE BEDS

Salvia officinalis 'Purpurascens' Evergreen shrub

Paeonia mlokosewitschii Perennial

Leycesteria formosa Deciduous shrub

Jasminum beesianum Evergreen shrub

Salvia involucrata 'Bethellii' Deciduous shrub

S. uliginosa Deciduous shrub

Bottom Rose Walk

Rosa 'Sander's White Rambler' Deciduous shrub

R 'Pink Perpétué' Deciduous shrub

R. 'Köln am Rhein' Deciduous shrub

R. Dublin Bay Deciduous shrub

R. Breath of Life Deciduous shrub

R. 'Bad Neuenahr' Deciduous shrub

R. 'Paul's Himalayan Musk' Deciduous shrub

R. 'White Cockade' Deciduous shrub

R. 'Morgengruss' Deciduous shrub

R. 'Elegance' Deciduous shrub

R. 'Rosy Mantle' Deciduous shrub

Jasminum x *stephanense* Deciduous climber

J. officinale Deciduous climber

Lonicera caprifolium Deciduous climber

L. x *americana* Deciduous climber

L. periclymenum 'Serotina' Deciduous climber

L. x *heckrottii* Deciduous climber

L. periclymenum 'Belgica' Deciduous climber

Clematis alpina 'Illusion' Deciduous climber

C. jouiana Deciduous climber

Vitis 'Brant' Deciduous climber

Acknowledgements

The authors would like to thank all those who have helped them in the preparation of this book. Particular thanks must go to David Howard, Dennis Brown, Gilly Hayward, Fred Ind and the other garden and estate staff. In addition, Richard Aylard, Julian and Isabel Bannerman, Willie Bertram, David Blissett, Caroline Clifton-Mogg, Charles Clover, Keith Critchlow, Deborah Devonshire, Andrew Donnington, Amanda Hornby, Mary Killen, David Magson, Charles Morris, Nick Mould, Amanda Packford-Garrett, Elizabeth-Ann Pile, Dick Reid, Miriam Rothschild, Mollie Salisbury, Erica-Mary Sanford, Sophia Spink, Roy Strong, Rosemary Verey, Jenny Whitaker and Giles Wood all provided much help, support and contributions, as did Stephen Lamport, Mark Bolland, Michael Fawcett, Bernie Flannery, Kevin Lomas, Lizzie Burgess, Millie Gray, Shona Williams, Elspeth Sigee and Annabel Cutbill from The Prince of Wales's Office.

The authors would like to extend especial thanks to Helena Attlee, Desmond Elliott, Susan Haynes, Kevin Knott, David Rowley, Nigel Soper and Rupert Lycett Green for their help and encouragement in the production of this book.

Index

Photographs by Andrew Lawson and Christopher Simon Sykes

Additional photographs:
David Rowley 3, 28, 32-33, 42, 50, 68 (bottom), 77(top), 95 (top), 95 (bottom), 118-119,125, 134, 143,172-173.
Nigel Soper 42 (bottom),151(top), 158 (bottom),161 (bottom).

Design director David Rowley
Designed by Nigel Soper
Editorial director Susan Haynes
Edited by Helena Attlee
Printed and bound in Italy by Printer Trento S.r.l.

www.stmartins.com

ISBN 0-312-27551-X

First published in the United Kingdom by Weidenfeld & Nicolson

First U.S. Edition

1 0 9 8 7 6 5 4 3 2

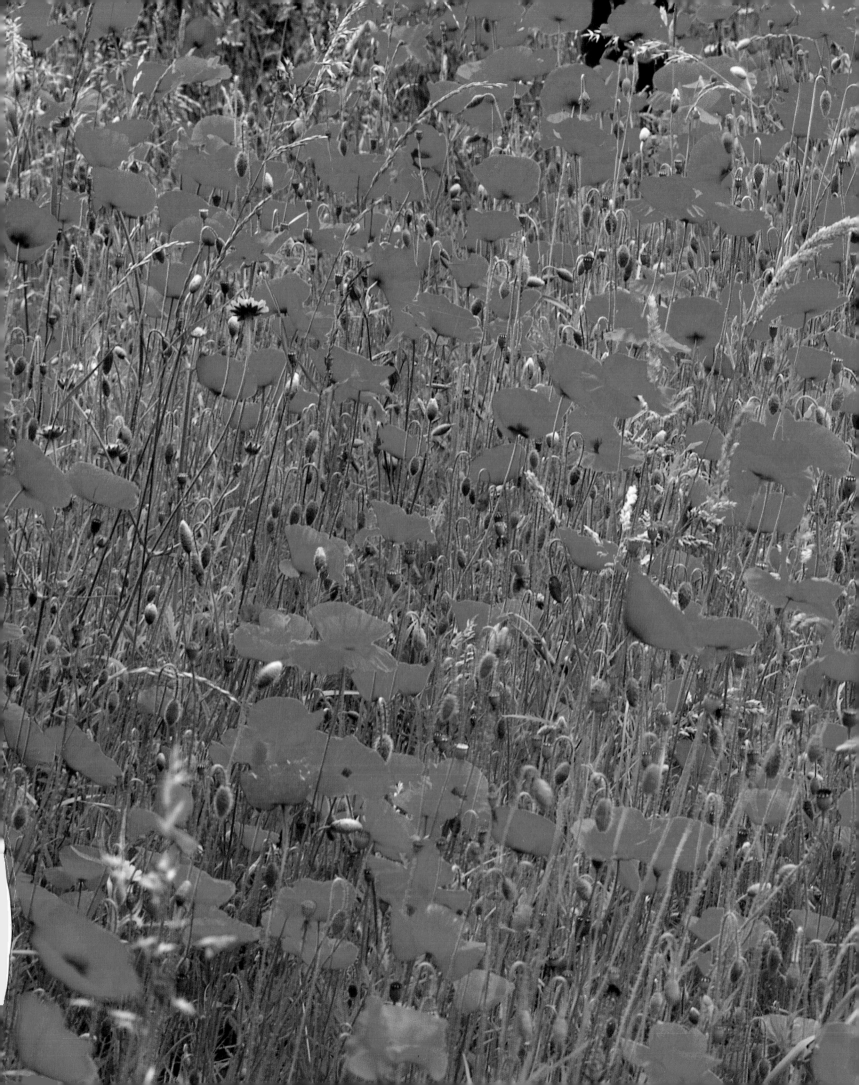